Charles and Me

Charles and Me

NOTES IN THE MARGIN

Pat Shannon

OPEN AIR

Published by
OPEN AIR, an imprint of
FOUR COURTS PRESS
c/o ISBS, 5824 N.E. Hassalo Street, Portland, OR 97213.

ACKNOWLEDGMENTS

The photograph by Izadore Bleckman on page 219 is © 1979 Izadore Bleckman
and printed with permission. 'The Instant Park' (pages 15–16 below) is from
On the Road with Charles Kuralt by Charles Kuralt, copyright © 1985 by CBS
Inc.; used by permission of G.P. Putnam's Sons, a division of Penguin Putnam
Inc. 'Dateline America' (pages 56–57 and 218–19 below) is 'Apache, Oklahoma'
and 'Chicago' for *Dateline America* by Charles Kuralt, copyright © 1979 by
Harcourt, Inc., reprinted by permission of the publisher.

ISBN 1–85182–718–8

Printed in Great Britain
by MPG Books Ltd, Bodmin, Cornwall.

To

John Charles Shannon
Born 1900   Died 1973
'You pays your money, and you takes your chances.'

Wanda Beatrice Shannon
Born 1908 (?)   Died 1994
'Where's the green beer?'

The woods are lovely, dark and deep.
But I have promises to keep,
And miles to go before I sleep ...

Robert Frost, 1923

But when the birds are gone, and their warm fields
Return no more, where, then, is paradise?

Wallace Stevens, 1923

Late at night when I am restless, I take an unframed picture down from the Derrynavglaun mantelpiece. I trace the images on the photo. It is from the early days. It is of a man surrounded by burnished metal and cut glass. He stands thoughtful, admiring, as the treasures gleam, dazzling, around him. I wait for him to speak. What will he have to say, I wonder, this quiet man with the serene air?

The picture fills me with bittersweet memories. It was taken in Reno, Nevada in 1971 by CBS cameraman Izadore Bleckman during the filming of an On The Road story Charles Kuralt was doing for the *CBS Evening News with Walter Cronkite*. Charles is standing amid the Harrah's Club automobile collection. Bill Harrah built the collection at the same time he was turning Harrah's Club into the most prosperous casino in northern Nevada. Bill Harrah loved gambling, but he loved those cars more. He said to anyone who would listen that he wanted them to stay in Reno, go up to the University of Nevada campus, maybe, find a permanent home in a building as elegant as the roadsters and touring cars themselves, sleek and powerful, carrying the dreams of a world that recognized no limits. Bill Harrah died, and his heirs dismantled the collection. They are gone, those cars, sold to the highest bidder. It is a pity and not what he wanted, but people do strange things when they are given riches, and see the chance for more.

Charles had an avaricious streak. Not for money. If Charles, the most tolerant of men, ever felt a twinge of contempt it was for those who stockpiled wealth, those fat cats. He couldn't see the point of it. It was movement that made him gluttonous. He sought the open road with as much fervor as a stock trader rakes in profits. Once on a winding drive up a lonely mountain pass, he said to me, I want it all. You're greedy, I complained. Yes, he agreed, smiling and happy. I am. I want it all.

It was chance that brought Charles and me together. Gambler's luck. Or, gambler's misfortune. In Nevada on any given day it may be either one or the other, or both. It was the summer of 1968, a time of turmoil, and, as CBS News legend Eric Sevareid pointed out, in the Western world upheavals are often a time of hope. It is the possibility of a better life that makes men restless. Revolution gives off an alluring scent. I caught a whiff and couldn't wait to stand up and be counted. Charles had been counted long ago. He was in Reno to get a story.

All that spring the kids and I sat on the sofa in our little house behind the big house watching Martin Luther King change our country, and as remote as we were out in the arid West we felt the despair at his death. I couldn't get it out of my mind. Every morning on my way to work as I drove past the county golf course on Arlington Avenue I would think of the black kids in the news, the kids without luxurious expanses of lawn to tumble on, the shady oasis of tall, shapely trees to dream under.

Reno, as segregated as the South, was home to a small contingent of African-Americans who lived in the northeast corner of town. An acre or so of land, vacant, weed-covered, sat untended in the middle of that neighborhood just off Oddie Boulevard. I saw it one day when I was prowling around wondering how you make friends with a black family. The lot was a disgrace as it was, but with a little work it would make a nice playground. I talked it over with my buddy, Don Dondero. We went out and took photographs in the neighborhood. There was one shot of children playing in a field that went straight to your heart. I persuaded an artist friend to do a mock-up of a flyer using the picture with the caption, 'A Day Late and A Dollar Short,' a phrase Daddy always used, the story of my family's life in a way. The idea was to sell shares for a dollar each and use the money to build a park.

Jimmy Sales, a genial ex-cop who found hustling promotions for the Sierra Pacific Power Company an easier way to make a living, had no qualms about putting the muscle on local business people. He introduced me around. I told everyone my great idea. They thought it was terrible. I needed a better hook. In the Sixties nothing seemed too outlandish, so I thought, why not build the park over a week-end? Get everything donated. Forget the solemnity. Reno is a fast town. Gamblers have short attention spans.

It worked. We called it the Instant Park. We had meetings. People showed up. In a couple of weeks we had a construction foreman, a nurseryman, a landscape architect, a contractor. A practical group. If I began waxing philosophical, they quieted me down and got back to business. In two months we were almost ready to go. We still needed an acre of sod, well, it wouldn't be instant if you sowed seed. No one stepped up to donate those green blocks, so I took out a loan at the credit union and hoped for the best. There was one problem I hadn't anticipated. We didn't seem to have the land. I thought that patch of ground was owned by the city. It wasn't. It was owned by the school district. The schoolboard was incredulous when they heard we expected them to give the plot to us. Said we weren't anybody so how could they, and, even if we were somebody, they weren't about to make a charitable donation. It wasn't legal. I went to the Reno city council. Asked them to buy the land. They were equally incredulous. We still didn't seem to be anybody.

I huddled with the committee. We agreed we needed publicity. Reno Newspapers was no help. The publisher told me frankly he had no interest in a park in a black neighborhood. The radio and television stations were sitting on their hands. Maybe, we should try for national coverage. I proposed calling Huntley and Brinkley at NBC to see if I could sell them on the story. Someone suggested CBS. The network was wrapping up its Friday night news with a segment called On The Road with Charles Kuralt. It sounded ready-made for us.

I called Walter Cronkite. Cronkite's secretary answered. A tactful woman she suggested that since Charles was in the office that day perhaps it would speed things along if I spoke to him directly, and she transferred the call. Charles picked up the phone.

The On The Road bus was a fixture of the American countryside over the next ten years, but Charles and the crew arrived in Reno on a Thursday night in a convoy of three immaculate, identical blue sedans; the bus, frequently on the fritz, had broken down in Salt Lake City. The four of them, a cameraman, lighting technician, sound engineer and newsman, checked into the old Holiday Hotel, then glitzy on the corner of Center Street and the Truckee River, anchoring the southern boundary of the gambling district.

I was frantic there would be a last minute slip-up. The network wouldn't do the piece after all. I pleaded with Charles to let me come by that evening to fill him in on what was going on. There was a mighty uproar in town. If the CBS crew didn't do the story I was going to be in a lot of trouble. The city council and the school board had dawdled for weeks over disposition of the land. Trying to hurry them along I sent telegrams urging action, eliciting a caustic reply from the head of the school system, a nice man who later insisted there would never have been a park if there hadn't been a patsy for a school superintendent. Charles was adamant; the crew was tired. They were going to bed early. I should pick him up the next morning, Friday, July 17th (my youngest daughter Shannon's ninth birthday) at 7 o'clock in front of the hotel. Charles didn't go to bed early at all. He stayed up all night playing roulette, stacking checks on 17, 21 and 27, his favorite numbers. Lost, too. Served him right.

The next morning my three kids and I drove up in our not too battered Volkswagen Bug. Charles was waiting curbside. Always at ease, he settled into the passenger seat as I whipped through town out to the park, talking non-stop, complaining vociferously about the CBS station whose news department was ignoring us and whose general manager was in my opinion a racist bastard. Charles told me not to worry. Everything would be fine.

Everything was fine, just like Charles said it would be.

That Sunday night after the last child left the park and before he went back on the road the following morning, Charles and I dined at a restaurant in the foothills overlooking the lights of the city, and then drove back down to the Holiday Hotel where we sat in the lounge and talked until dawn. He arrived at my door barely visible behind a billow of roses, crimson, long-stemmed, which Mother thrust into a bucket of water for lack of a Baccarat vase. I can't recall whether Charles was early or I was late, but Mother welcomed him while my children, Kathleen, J.R. and Shannon, eyed him from across the room. I do remember looking at him as I walked down the small hallway, and I remember Charles rising from the overstuffed chair, looking at me. I was wearing my best dress, a navy blue crepe, long sleeves snug at the wrist, billowing skirt, round neckline outlined with pearls. He, even then rumpled in the blue blazer with gold buttons, the dark slacks, clones of which he wore until his death, was the most attractive man I had ever seen. I am still puzzled and a little irritated when Charles is described as balding and pudgy, adjectives that never come to mind when I think of him. I think quiet wit, amused look, eager camaraderie, quick intelligence.

In covering the park Charles had discovered just about all there was to know about me. I hailed from a small family of nomads, clannish and close, whose goodbyes were meant to be permanent and whose returns were rare and unexpected. I was a single mother, divorced, and living alone with my children. Being broke and in debt was as certain for me as catching a face card if you draw to a ten and a six.

That night Charles told me about himself, growing up in North Carolina, marrying his college sweetheart, Sory Guthrie, the move to Brooklyn when he went to work for CBS. During brief periods at home he would take his daughter Lisa on walks, and she would say good morning to a statue of a great man whose name I have forgotten, and once when he was playing checkers with her, she began to cry she was losing so badly, and Sory said, for god's sake, Charles, she's only three. Sory, Charles explained, had been lonely and unhappy while he traveled the world. After five years of marriage, Sory took the girls and went back to North Carolina and a sensible life. Charles agreed to let Sory's new husband adopt the girls, but sent big checks anyway though they were never quite enough. He told me about his current wife, Petie Baird, a former CBS secretary, and the slow ebbing of that marriage which over the years became companionable but never ended. He told me about broadcasting basketball games when he was a kid and reporting for the *Charlotte News* and being editor of the University of North Carolina *Tar Heel* and about his father, Pops, who said you had to leave things better than the way you found them.

As the night ended Charles drove me home under the disappearing stars promising to return in September. No, I said. I know how the world works. People don't come back. They keep going. Later in the morning when I picked up the Bug parked in the hotel lot, there was a note stuck under the windshield wiper. On the outside of a small cardboard folder, the kind that once held two postage stamps, was written, 'people do say goodbye'; on the inside, 'and then hello.'

ON THE ROAD: THE INSTANT PARK

A vacant lot in Reno, Nevada. 7:35 a.m. on a Friday morning in a town not noted for early risers. But one group of men has been up since before dawn, and now they gather at a surveyor's table. This block of land, in a largely Negro neighborhood, has always been a vacant lot. These men, contractors, builders, are going to turn it into a park, with walks and grass and trees and basketball courts and places to rest in the shade. They are going to do it without charge, and they're going to do it in the next 48 hours.

Contractor Tony Taormina sends his son Chris out to check a surveyor's stake, and the work is on.

By 8:30 a.m., two thousand tons of top soil, which came free, is being spread by big front-end loaders, which were also contributed, operated by heavy equipment men, union men, not used to working for nothing—working for nothing.

By 9:30, the lot is filled with other people, who never met before today and who have nothing in common except that they all think this vacant lot ought to be a park. Bill Brooks, a school custodian ... Lonnie Femster, an unemployed kid ... and Manny Ruiz, a roofer by trade ... are digging the same ditch. Gee Hardadge, 84 years old, who came by to watch, picks up a shovel and gets down in the ditch himself. He says he needs the exercise.

You have to remind yourself that this is Reno, a town which makes divorcees out of married couples, and marks out of strangers, and has never been widely recognized for generosity and compassion.

You get the feeling that something extraordinary is happening on this vacant lot. Guy Smith, a mechanic has the same feeling.

Throughout the long day, 'Red', who is Len Lewis, keeps sawing as if everything depended on him alone.

Almost lost in this crowd is a slight, pretty woman named Pat Shannon Baker. The whole crazy idea of building a park in two days was hers. The night Martin Luther King was killed, she sat up late, as so many people did … thinking the things so many people thought … thinking she had to do something. The difference between Pat Baker and most other people is that after talking to her employer, the Sierra Pacific Power Company, and to people in the neighborhood, and to tough-minded contractors she'd never met before, she was able to figure out what to do. Her idea became theirs, too, and now they're pouring concrete, and Pat Baker is watching her dream happen out here in the sun.

By Saturday morning at 10, the dream is there to be seen in outline. Coast guardsmen, marines, Seabees are pitching in. A little girl named Donna Snow plans to work all day doing what she can do, carrying water.

Saturday night in Reno was always a night for bright lights and action. In this corner of town, these are the bright lights, and this is the action.

And now it's Sunday afternoon, and there's a park here, and it's time to dedicate it. They named it Pat Baker Park.

The park is here, and it will be a good thing for this neighborhood, which needed a park. A black man leaning on a shovel when it was done, said, 'This is the only good thing that's happened in Reno since I've been here, 14 years.'

He didn't mean the park. He meant—building the park.

Charles Kuralt, CBS News, Reno, Nevada.

The sinuous twistings and turnings that brought my family to rest in the city of trembling leaves resembles the trail of a diamond-backed rattler gliding down an alkali gully on a hot summer's day, most times stretched and easy, then, suddenly, a pause, a circle. A rattlesnake coils when alarmed; an independent, ornery cuss, he is happiest going his own way leaving a wide berth between himself and strangers, but he'll fight when backed into a corner. That's sort of the way we were. Maybe, still are.

Nevada is an hospitable place for people wary of strangers. There isn't a lot of poking and prodding. It's a good place to hole up. I called Reno home, no matter where we were, ever since my family landed there just before World War II when I was a kid of seven. It was the center to which I was always drawn back, but in 1963 I was back with no money and three small children.

I went to work shilling on the midnight shift for Clete Libby at the Cal-Neva Club, corner of Center and Second. Shills played a desultory game of cards with the dealer on empty Twenty-one tables until an unwary tourist put up real money. Then, after a hand or two, they drifted away to drink coffee until another table was emptied. To be a shill you didn't fill out any personnel forms. You didn't need any experience. You started right away. You got paid in cash at the end of the shift. Not bad if you were down on your luck.

Born on a crap table in one of the cow counties, Clete Libby knew all there was to know about gambling. A pit boss covering the midnight shift had to know everything. The raucous, evening mobs begging the house to take their twenty dollar bills were easy. Cautious daytime bettors with an allotted one hundred dollars, willing to take a ten percent return and not unhappy if they broke even, were boring, but certain.

Serious gamblers ambled in at three or four in the morning when the tables were empty. They went head to head, pitting their counting of the cards with the dealer's right to break and shuffle. Single decks were the rule. No one in his right mind played with a double deck. Triple decks were such an obvious ploy to the gullible, no casino even considered it. The pit boss's job was to make sure the game was honest— or dishonest—depending on the club. No stacking of the deck, no marking of the cards, no false shuffle, no flashing, no accomplice. Libby could watch the pit from the bar and tell what was going on. He knew all the motions. Years later, when I dealt for Harrah's, the store had a squad of young men huddling around any table where a dealer lost a few hands and another battalion upstairs crouched behind one-way mirrors. If one of the boys was lucky, he might spot a false move. But, probably not.

In everything but gambling, Libby was medium. Medium height. Medium build. Medium coloring. He wore his hair parted on the side and sleeked back. He had a wide mouth with narrow lips and wore horn-rimmed glasses. He drove to work in a Chrysler sedan as buffed and polished as his finger nails. He arrived wearing a fedora and topcoat over a tailored brown suit. He was a piece of work. And, he was easy. He taught me to deal Twenty-one.

It was a trial at first. I was nervous and clumsy. The cards, wet with perspiration, clumped together when I shuffled. Libby attacked the problem from a variety of angles. He believed I was clumsy because I was tired all the time. He gave me large, chalky vitamin tablets to build up my strength. To counteract drowsiness he gave me tiny, sleek, yellow pills of unknown composition. To calm my nerves, I drank brandy and coffee during the twenty minute breaks which followed the forty minutes on the table. As a final precaution, Libby gave me a can of baby powder. A light sprinkling on the cards and a brushing across the palms smoothed out the shuffling.

Early one morning a high roller from back east slumped over a whiskey at the bar canvassed the action in the pit. After a few minutes of mild concentration, he pushed back and approached my table. I had developed one eccentricity. Instead of spreading the cards in a smooth, fast break in front of the check holder, I swiped them in an arc when the table was dead. The arc appealed to him. Fastidious in dress and soft of hand, the gambler reached into his pocket and pulled out a wad of bills, straightened them carefully, laid them on the green felt of my table. I swooped up the deck in my right hand, gave it a sharp tap, neatly pulled it into two even piles, riffled my fingers across the edges of the cards. A perfumed white cloud rose into the air. The gambler stared in disbelief, for a brief moment, too stunned to act. His manicured hand reached for his money. His gaze brushed Libby's blank stare before he turned and walked out the door. No one spoke a word.

Libby was one of the great teachers of the world. You're not swimming, he'd point out complacently. Keep your elbows in, stop flailing your arms, flip the cards. His idea of dealing was a graceful ballet, full of ease and fluidity, under perfect control. If you dealt like Libby told you to, gamblers could be mesmerized by the beauty of the motion and stolen from with a light touch. That was the whole point. Not for use everyday, of course, but if the occasion should arise, you were covered. First, your arms were relaxed, elbows at your sides, hands and deck close to your chest. Your left hand held the deck high, the forefinger shielding the top of deck in case it had been marked. The palm of the right hand rested against the bottom of the deck, fingers curved down. Same reason. When dealing out the cards, the left thumb pushed the top card off the deck at a slight angle. The barest tip of the card is caught between the thumb and the forefinger of the right hand, and the card is sent in a fast spin to the player with a flip of the middle finger. The movement, small, scarcely noticeable, makes it possible for a nimble dealer to send the second card across the table as easily as the top one, and none the wiser.

After the cards are fanned neatly around the table, the dealer drops her hands in a casual stance with the deck top turned toward her. A simple flick of the thumb, a quick turn inward of the wrist and the top card is revealed. Handy. Both hands are used in paying or collecting checks, turning over all the cards at once, messily, rapidly, talking, laughing, stacking the cards as you go. Then the shuffle, a clean pull through if the deck is stacked, a delightful riffle, one on one, if you're just doing a good job. This was the style that made the bean counters fall out of the ceiling at Harrah's when the businessmen stole gambling from the gamblers.

In the Sixties the clubs were pretty honest. Occasionally, they would dump. Just a few friends picking up a little on the side. Sometime after I left the Cal-Neva, dealing at a club I'll not finger, I was moved to a table to sign a fill after the last check had been sent to the other side. The rationale, correct as it turned out, was that if accounting took notice, they would see who had signed, know it was a new dealer and let it go.

The casino was a good place for me. There were drawbacks. No worker perks. No medical insurance or paid holidays or guarantee you would make it through the shift. If a dealer blew a table once too often on a night the pit boss was feeling particularly gloomy, he'd yank you out of the pit. You'd be walking out the door with your pay in your hand before you had time to complain, or what was more likely, be sitting at the bar grimly drinking and muttering darkly. If business was slow, you'd be sent home early, or get a call just before your shift began, telling you to forget it. If business was good, you could pull sixteen hours and never mind complaining. On the other hand if the boss rubbed you wrong, there was always another joint up the street. The pay wasn't terrific, but a friendly dealer could rack up the tips. You kept what you made. No splitting with the grouches.

I left Libby without a backward glance and moved to the Bank Club when I heard it was paying a couple more dollars a shift. The old Bank had been one of the seediest places in town, but new owners took over the hotel as well as the casino and decided to go upscale. Old-timers like Libby scoffed at the idea that show biz in the pit would increase a night's take and watched the proceedings with disdain. Under their scornful gaze, the Bank Club metamorphosed into a saloon straight out of *The River of No Return*. Not for its dealers the onerous chore of trotting to the local uniform shop for mundane purchases of off-the-rack black and white. We had fitting rooms and dressmakers. On my first evening at work I was sewn into a velvet gown, emerald green, gored skirt, bare shoulders. They put feathers in my hair and green shadow on my eyelids. I was something to see. In the middle of the casino floor a brass periscope put in an unexpected appearance; a barely visible naked girl on the proverbial red velvet swing waved to inquisitive viewers from a tiny room located between the gas mains and the water pipes in the basement. In the club lounge, tough mamas belted out, 'I don't want him, you can have him, he didn't love me anyway ... ,' and good family folk sat at ringside tables ogling half-clad beauties in the show room.

The pit was down home, rude and rough. Tillie Stillion was the casino manager. Rumor had it he was part of the mob. I don't know about that, but shortly after the hotel opened a fire sent Tillie dashing from table to table gathering up drop boxes as the rest of us dodged fire hoses and ladders. He was not one to mix up his priorities. Tillie fired me when I made the mistake of asking for more overtime. His reasoning was simple. A dealer needing money was a dealer tempted to steal. End of story.

For me the vaudevillian days of the casino were spluttering out. I'd done my walk-on in about a thousand performances, including matinees, but before the curtain dropped, I hired on for one last engagement at the Spark's Nugget. Dick Gregory was headlining the big room. He was a gambler back then. Loved the crap table. On a winning streak one night after the late show, with a gaggle of green floor managers around him, he paused before throwing the dice and looked around with that dead pan gaze, 'This is the first time I've had so many white boys worrying about the state of my health.'

These were the years Charles was recovering from a dazzling rise and fall at CBS News. He was hired away from the Charlotte News in Charlotte, North Carolina in 1957 as a news writer for WCBS Radio in New York. Within months he was pulled over to CBS Television to write the *CBS Evening News with Douglas Edwards.* In 1960 he became the youngest CBS News correspondent and as roving anchor for the top-rated *Eyewitness to History* was launched on a dizzying trajectory around the world covering the week's top news story. He was kicked off the show by the then head of CBS television who thought him too low-key and shipped off to Latin America.

We might have met, but didn't, when Charles returned to the States in 1963 to head up the CBS Los Angeles bureau. Bob Laxalt, a writer and friend from my University of Nevada days and brother of soon-to-be governor, Paul Laxalt, persuaded Mark Curtis to hire me as a copywriter for a new advertising and public relations firm, Tyson-Curtis Advertising. Mark, a shy, extremely funny man, was a great believer in institutions as an avenue for progress. At the moment his interest lay in upgrading the rowdy Nevada press corps. Toward that end, he became one of the sires of the Reno Press Club. A wild and occasionally professional crowd of reporters, attorneys, politicians and hangers-on intrigued behind a door opening off a back corridor in the Riverside Hotel which was signed by the Press Club's high-crowned Stetson hat.

Two disparate news stories brought Charles to Reno propelling him into the disorderly rooms hidden behind the Stetson. The first revolved around the kidnapping of Frank Sinatra's son. The second time Charles came to the Reno Press Club it was to cover Barry Goldwater who used the venue to deliver a policy speech during his run for the presidency in 1964. The Sinatra story didn't interest me, but I was bewitched by politics and was atremble to hear what clap of thunder Goldwater would send roiling over this most conservative of audiences. I didn't make the Goldwater luncheon speech. Our family came down with chickenpox, tumbling in forlorn little heaps, one after the other, Kathleen, Shannon, J.R. and me. We would have died, probably, if it hadn't been for the kindness of the Tyson-Curtis art director and our best friend, Edna Huntford, who left a pot of chicken soup on the front doorstep before hurrying off to claim her seat at the groaning board.

So, I missed my chance. But I see him now, young, smiling, lusting for life. My Charles.

I had been divorced for five years, and Charles was on his second marriage, when we met. I was thirty-four; he was thirty-three. Between us we had five young children, three at home, two away. Both sets of our parents were ever present in our lives, mine physically attendant each day; his no less intimately involved though often thousands of miles distant. How could we have been so cheerful about our prospects? So optimistic? So light-hearted? Now, forced to look back on our actions—which I never questioned at the time—and to try to explain them, I cannot come up with a construction with which I am happy. Europeans are more sanguine about the heart's contrariness, so I fall back on the Irish poet Patrick Kavanagh who wrote:

I saw the danger, yet I walked along the enchanted way,
And I said, let grief be a fallen leaf at the dawning of the day.

Charles, a master at not answering the question that was asked but answering, instead, the question he wanted asked, would have laughed at the query—why did they do it, those two, that courtly Southerner and that bold Nevada broad?—while locking me in his amused gaze: 'They don't know, do they, baby?'

Charles called every day during the six weeks following the park. He was subbing for Cronkite on the evening news that August and one weekend languished in his office bracing for the fall of Czechoslovakia. 'Dubcek! Dubcek! Dubcek!' We were mesmerized with misery. He sent a gold Dunhill lighter engraved PSB. I do not smoke, but this most observant of newsmen assumed, not for the last time, that we were one and the same. Sometimes we were. *Gentle Wilderness*, a paean to the Sierras, arrived in the mail with instructions, 'Pick a place, and we'll go there.'

Charles began our vacation by giving a speech to the Reno Chamber of Commerce. Sierra Pacific Power Company's invitation was open-ended. They were delighted when he readily agreed on a date for the first of September. The business community was miffed that Charles had called Reno a town not widely recognized for generosity and compassion and were looking for an apology. They didn't get it. Charles was mindful of his writing and meant what he said. He didn't care for retractions. He arrived with a typed speech lauding grass roots' movements. In the Sixties sensible ideas originated with the people, not with government or institutions. He cited the environmentalist, the feminist, the civil rights marcher as cases in point. That speech and that piece of paper survived for years as Charles changed the name, Reno Chamber of Commerce, to, perhaps, a library group in Mississippi, and the opening lines from an appreciation of the high Sierras to a line of Mark Twain's on the Mississippi River. In the car on the way to auditorium or hotel, Charles would pull the top off of a favorite broad-tipped pen, securing the cap between his teeth as he rapidly changed words and phrases before jumping out curbside into an anxious covey of hosts.

The day after his speech to the Reno Chamber of Commerce, Charles and I backpacked into the Desolation area high above the Sierra Nevada tree line. That morning before we left I flipped through my three cookbooks, *Fanny Farmer*, an early Spice Islands classic and *Sunset Magazine*'s offering of exotic meals, seeking a breakfast menu befitting the moment settling on a hangtown fry as just the thing: Western, hearty, vaguely daring. Charles washed down the sizzling oysters with gulps of a blazing Bloody Mary. We stuffed our backpacks with scotch and brandy, a few bottles of decent wine, cans of Denty Moore stew, a box of pancake mix and strode out leaving Mother to watch over the children, already enrolled in fall classes, and to fervently hope we would make it back in one piece.

The trail not so worn as it is these days, drenched with pine needles, disappearing up craggy canyons, erupting into wild glens, cut across a churning stream. I inched along a fallen log as Charles waded waist deep in the snow melt. Hold my hand, he said. On the far side of the waters a magical kingdom awaited us, a kingdom which would advance and recede over the years as Charles conjured up fabulous entertainments to amuse and delight, opened doors into new worlds where without him the children and I were lost among the wonders, adrift, shy and confused, waiting for his return. He burst into our shattered lives, bags bulging with gifts, morels from Michigan, bright blue shopping bags from Kyoto, amber beads from Russia, telling stories, playing games, planning adventures, pooh-poohing gloom. Even the abysses held terrors colored and contorted by spirits not of this world. From those first heady moments to this day Charles has informed every moment of my life. Serene, giddy, maniacal, raging, sunk in depression, ecstatic, it didn't matter. He was always there, steady, sure, unwavering and unmoveable.

That first day we pitched our tent beside a crystal clear lake. Charles assembled his fly rod and went to catch dinner. A neophyte at the game he approached fly fishing as he did every endeavor with a seriousness of purpose steeped in intellectual confidence. He knew the history, read all the books, talked to the experts, watched the best, sized up his own talents, set a place for himself, and straight as a good cast went right to the mark. We ate a rainbow trout for dinner that night. Forget the Denty Moore stew.

For the next few years Charles and I romped through the Sierras gradually easing out of our pup tent into rough fishing cabins or comfortable country inns, giving up the thrill of stream bathing for lashings of hot water. We had grown accustomed to one another and took life a little easier, not needing to shine every moment, happy to relax and let life go as life must. The two of us slipped away each September, but August was family month. Charles flew in at odd moments joining the kids and me, lazy on a Lake Tahoe beach. I felt a thrill of ordinariness one year when we discovered within a built-in seat-box the mate to a pair of Charles' freshly-shined black shoes, gone missing the year before.

My children lost their father to the ravages of divorce. Now, when they were least expecting it, a replacement arrived. My own father tried to take up the slack in the children's lives after my divorce providing them with an unfailingly sympathetic male point of view. When I was growing up Daddy set the tenor of our lives. Mother was the canvas, Daddy the streak of color, so he fell into the job naturally. He was a good father and a good grandfather though a little erratic. His people were settlers, men and women revered as heroes by one generation and reviled as murders by the next. Pioneers! O Pioneers! Whatever they were, they held the family to be sacrosanct. His mother and father raised him in an adoring circle of aunts and uncles and grandmothers and grandfathers in a small Nebraska town. They lived a quiet, decent life as far as I can tell. My grandfather ran a small business, advertising 'Sanitary plumbing in all its forms, common sense heating in all its forms, and practical lighting in many forms … ' My grandmother's signature appears in a list of forty conveners of Ravenna's First Congregational Church. That was back in 1886. Daddy, born in 1900, was cosseted and coddled and couldn't wait to get away.

Daddy chased gold through the deserts of the Southwest, first alone, then with Mother and me and my sister, opening and closing auto body shops in one dusty Western town after another trying to get enough money together for a stake. Daddy never found the Mother Lode. The Superstitions, Searchlight, the Lost Dutchman. Chimeras, all. Daddy's dybbuk led him away from the enchanted lands, dragging him north to Nevada. The vengeful spirit robbed him of his ardor, teased and taunted and haunted him for the rest of his days, granting him no rest, and Mother no relief. Still, he loved us, always, took care of us in his fashion and gave me a view of life that I find as valid today as when he first undertook my education when I was a child.

That education, a rambling affair, was under his firm if sporadic guidance. Reading was restricted. No comic books allowed. He led me by the hand to the Washoe County library at the back of the old Pioneer Theater in downtown Reno depositing me with the librarian, trusting she would keep me on the straight and narrow. He approved of the arts in principal, but his preferences were informed more by nostalgia for the gentle ways of his parents than by personal choice. He was partial to parlor songs. '*Only a Rose*' was a favorite. I would painstakingly pick out the melody on an old upright as he sang, a quavering, nasal rendition oddly reminiscent of the Irish *sean-nós* singer.

Daddy's stand on religion was unequivocal, if a little muddled. He was not going to allow anyone to lead me down the primrose path of easy salvation. He was skeptical of claims to arcane knowledge to which he was not privy. On the other hand he was temperamentally disposed to the chaste and tender sound of childish hymns and to being dressed in one's Sunday best while contributing generously to the collection plate. He encouraged me to believe in the simple Christian virtues of speaking out for the Indians and siding with the unions while expressly forbidding forays into supernatural belief. Christmas pageants and Easter bonnets were in; catechism was out. Needless to say, I was never baptized.

When Charles found us a generation later, I was raising my children much as Mother and Daddy raised me. In a curious blend of their roles, I proved better at providing shelter than soothing bruised egos. I was a pretty good father, but not a very good mother. If Charles could have stayed still, he would have been a gifted father. He was a loving and respectful man. He listened. He gave sound advice grounded in a deeply humanist approach to life. Charles tried to fashion a platform of reality under our swooping flight through the ether. Assuming a melancholy visage I would read the children Nietzsche, 'man is but an ape between man and superman.' Charles couldn't bear it. He would grab a copy of *Winnie the Poo*, 'Imagine that, the man was fat, nicknamed The Handsome.' But, he couldn't stay still, so he became the world's best uncle, our Drosselmeir. The children didn't care about the label. For them whatever he was, whoever he was, he was the best.

J.R.'s bruising encounters at Pop Warner football were eased by Charles's pep talks and thoughts of defeat erased by games of pepper played in the back yard. A scorecard kept with red and green markers snuggles next to other family valuables in an oblong wicker basket commandeered years ago, just for the moment, until something more suitable could be found. Over time the basket itself has become a family treasure. Charles eulogized Kathleen's cheerleading at Reno High with a spectacular photo blow-up for her bedroom wall, she miles off the ground, knees bent, arms outstretched. He and Shannon banged out duets on her new spinet. A breezy *Sentimental Journey* drifted down the canal back of the house, Charles sitting sideways on the bench, toe tapping, rocking on the base; Shannon, blond ponytail bouncing, carrying the melody.

Our lives overflowed with projects. Charles couldn't let a day go by without some small triumph to savor. Plans inevitably included raids on neighborhood shops, loading carts and arms with provisions. At Thanksgiving he stepped off the plane with a recipe for Thompson's turkey in his hand. We plundered the supermarket for sage and dry mustard and soy and honey and a fat turkey hen. Incredulous, we watched him mix unappetizing concoctions, daubing on layer after layer of spices and pastes until the poor hen was unrecognizable, and we were left groaning and sticking out our tongues, aghhhhh. He shoved the bird into the oven and left it there until it was charred, jubilantly removing the burnt layers to reveal the moistest, tastiest turkey we could ever have hoped to eat.

At Christmas we gathered around our scarred table, unrecognizable under its scraps of old lace, pipe cleaners, square jars of lacquer paints and silver sequins, creating whimsical tree ornaments. I still have Daddy's green pipe cleaner leprechaun in his Styrofoam hat waving a tiny clay pipe. Others, fragile as the day, are lost. We celebrated Easter, etching delicate Fabergé eggs, knitting our brows and narrowing our eyes, worrying over the complicated, satisfying process of stiletto designs and layered waxes and brilliant jewel-like hues.

Picnics acquired a certain formal charm. We carried a wicker hamper topped with a red and white cloth as we rustled through crackling leaves in the fall or gathered wildflowers in the spring. Friends passing by, laden with metal-framed backpacks, reacted doubtfully to Charles's urging, 'Would you care for a glass of champagne?' A photo of J.R.'s from that time captures a dubious moment: Charles, handsome; me, pensive. The story of our lives, Charles said: 'Me eating. You brooding.'

I had left Tyson-Curtis Advertising and was working for Sierra Pacific Power Company when Pat Baker Park was built. Soon after the park, I left the power company to work for Governor Paul Laxalt in Carson City, a half an hour commute from Reno, as a public information officer nee flack. I left Tyson-Curtis and, then Sierra Pacific, for the same reason I left Clete Libby at the Cal Neva. I was offered a slightly bigger paycheck. One would think with these constant job changes our family finances would rest solidly in the black. No such luck. That first September after the park, Charles arrived in Reno to discover a bounced check waiting for him along with his room reservation at the River House, a small inn situated on the Truckee River which its wealthy owner had done up in a simple but elegant Chinese fashion.

The returned check was mine, a room deposit in the amount of fifteen dollars, a respectable sum for me in those days, a check I hoped the bank would cover. It was a constant struggle to stay even. I fret about those years each time I hear someone complaining about single mothers on welfare. I worked all the time, sometimes dealing Twenty-one on the weekends or at night in addition to my nine-to-five. We still barely made it. Creditors were always after me. When I was dealing at Barney's up at Lake Tahoe, a friend of mine and I would exchange personal checks each Sunday before I drove back down the hill. She would deposit my check in her bank at the South Shore. I would deposit hers in Reno. This was before the cursed computer. It took a week for bank processing to take place. By then our paychecks had been deposited. In effect we lived on interest-free loans for the better part of a year. Without that bit of chicanery added to the fact that Mother and Daddy picked up much of the child care, I don't know what would have happened to us.

Governor Laxalt hired me, an eager political naïf, because of the park, a momentarily high-profile woman sympathetic to the civil rights movement. Still mourning the loss of Hubert Humphrey, I was a bit of an oddity in a Republican stronghold, but Paul welcomed me to the fold. He referred to me as the nanny of the cabinet when we were in the cow counties, that is not Reno or Las Vegas, and used me to dispatch liberal malcontents with a mild gibe. 'Patty is against the death penalty,' he would say innocently, 'You might want to talk to her about that.' Paul's ideas on a welfare state meshed with Daddy's. Neither had any use for an interfering government. They both believed in the family as the place of last resort where they 'have to let you in.' Years later when Paul was challenged on a political appointment—nepotism was the charge—the reply came from his heart: If you don't take care of your own, who will?

As I bumped along the cow paths of Nevada politics, Charles was making the fateful slide from brilliant reporter to glittering star. The first black cloud of celebrity lay low on the distant horizon, unnoticed by us. I remember one bright morning in Baja walking dreamily over a vividly patterned mosaic floor, watching the sea through an endless flow of white arches, when an American couple called out to us. 'You're Sandy Vanocur, aren't you?' 'Wrong network,' chided Charles.

In Carson City, Paul, soon bored as governor, decided not to run again. Taking care of his own, he sent me off to the Labor Department in San Francisco, public information officer, region nine. Charles arranged a dizzying week in the Bay Area to get us acclimatized. He sent us pin-wheeling down Lombard's hairpin curves, dancing at the ends of cable car straps to the jangled tat-a-ta-tat-a-ta-tat of the brass bell and pressed our reluctant noses against smudged windows where the pressed duck hung. To remind us the countryside still existed, Charles raced Shannon down misty paths weaving through stands of ancient redwoods before we finished the day chomping hamburgers on Sam's deck in Tiburon as we ogled sailboats tying up at the pier.

We scarcely exhausted the pros and cons of moving before Charles packed us into two cars, he taking the wheel of one, me the other, convoying to our new home across the Bay in Marin County. He got into Reno the day before the movers were to arrive to discover the four of us surrounded by empty packing boxes quarreling over what should go and what should be left behind. As was usual with Charles, he didn't chastise us, he just began throwing things pell-mell into cartons. J.R.'s rock collection, Kathleen's cheerleading mementos, Shannon's crayon drawings, my half-empty jars of spices. By midnight we were ready to go.

Our lives were taking on a new rhythm. The courtship was over. Nest building had begun. We rented a house in affluent Belvedere across the Golden Gate bridge. Our neighbors were mostly friendly, old-school types living quiet, peaceful existences just a bit above the fray. What must they have thought when we arrived? Mother doubtful, Daddy quite drunk, Shannon eager, Kathleen depressed, J.R. happy anywhere Charles was, our cat Playful vexed and her litter of kittens mewling, me on an adrenaline high, Charles making it all easy.

Our Poem of Thanksgiving

We are glad to have each other—
Mother and her own sweet mother;
Shannon, Kathleen, and their brother;
Jack and I, all here once more

Now we meet to slake our thirst
and eat until our tummies burst
with thoughts of Thomas Edward Harris First
and other things we're grateful for

Like Room 19, Mirador Motel,
to which tonight we say farewell
after a slightly overcrowded spell
of 60 days and nights

With yo ho, ho, a bottle of rum,
a drum roll on a big bass drum,
it's California here we come,
new smells and sounds and sights

We're thankful for Eucalyptus Road,
the site of our prepared abode,
and thankful for the mover's load
and hope that it arrives

We've got lots of bills, mostly Pat's
and four warm coats and at least 4 hats
and a little car and lots of cats
and each cat has 9 lives

So that's a lot of things we own
and if we pare things to the bone
and forego lights and a telephone
and see our chance and take it

And if we live by the Golden Rule
and keep the kids out of school
and eat only milk and gruel
then we may just barely make it.

We offer thanks for the things we share
for Kathleen's smile and Shannon's hair
and J.R.'s joyful lack of care
that always keeps us guessing

And most of all, our thanks for Pat,
who loves us all; knowing that
keeps us together. It is Pat who
gives us our special blessing.

So we close our eyes and throw the dice
and pray that life turns out as nice
as our yams and turkey and wild rice.
Tonight, again, we're living.

*We thanks for life before we sup
And thanks for what is in our cup
And thanks for love we give up
On the evening of Thanksgiving.*

He tempted me with the perfection of a seven-minute boiled egg, the sleek white oval glistening in a thick, yellow glaze, and he beguiled me with the satisfactions of a *New York Times*'s crossword well done. 'You can get this one,' he would say, 'It's easy.' He filled the house with cascading falls of white daisies, as uncomplicated as the stories he told. He left messages: 'DEAR PAT Gone to town, so just sit aroun' and I'll come home to you! (with piano notes in treble), softly.' When I despaired at the drowning sea or flailed at the flaying winds, he tried as a patient parent to calm me. Seek friendlier shores, lie still until the storm plays out. I hear his voice as I tend my roses, rarely pausing, now, to remark on the dark, rushing clouds.

Charles was On The Road and only home every two to three weeks. He flew in late in the afternoon or early evening. I'd drive across the Golden Gate bridge cutting across the edge of San Francisco on Nineteenth to I-280 to the airport to pick him up. Singing loudly in an off-key sort of mewl, I would pirouette through the open-air parking on the top floor of the garage to watch the plane land. On the way back to Marin, exuberant, exhausted, full of talk, Charles read newspaper clippings aloud, pointed out witty or outlandish bumper stickers—'Insanity is Hereditary, You

Get It From Your Kids'—'Nuke The Whales'—'Eat Right, Exercise, Die Anyway'—admired the City, jeered at the joggers, squeezed my hand.

While I scrambled eggs and toasted sourdough we worried about the kids and Mother and Daddy and his mother and his father and his kids and On The Road and Able Baker Charlie Dog and his dog, Ralph. After dinner Charles would rummage through his bag pulling out the new Roger Angell baseball wrap-up or Freeman Dyson's latest science piece, reading, until I dozed off, no longer able to keep my eyes open, always sleepy, always ready to give up before him. He would pause. The silence would wake me.

'You were asleep.'

'No, I wasn't.'

'Yes, you were.'

The mornings were lazy. Charles sat on the edge of the bed in his ribbed cotton undershirt, one leg drawn up under him, looking out the window, smoking a cigarette, admiring a humming bird or watching Arachne spin a web. The radio would be tuned to the local news. I'd bring in juice. Then, coffee. Then, the paper. We'd inch into the dining room. If Mother was with us, she'd plunge her hands into our biggest mixing bowl transforming clouds of flour and cups of butter into the light-as-air sour cream biscuits that Charles loved and which I was never able to replicate. Charles carved off paper-thin slices of country ham. I'd put on North Carolina stone-ground grits and more eggs, this time, the seven minute kind. When Mother wasn't around, I'd stir up sour cream waffles or the world's best pancakes, a recipe of Mr. Kuralt's using whole kernel corn. If the kids didn't have an afternoon class, one or another would come home to find us still in our robes, sitting on the deck, doing the crossword, piles of dishes pushed to one side, coffee cups half-full.

Afternoons we might climb into the car for a drive up to Bodega Bay and eat cracked crab or meander through the wine country stopping to applaud a blacksmith at work. Maybe, instead of going by land, we would go by sea. Once, caught in a sudden, fierce storm while sailing around Angel Island, Kathleen and I watched masts breaking and booms jibing as Charles shouted orders to J.R. working the sails. I was unconcerned until Charles suddenly turned and shouted at me to keep my eyes on J.R. and keep pointing at him, no matter what, if he fell into the water. I never recognized danger when Charles was around unless he spelled it out for me.

At night we cooked, running down to the Boardwalk before closing to buy ingredients for lasagna, shaking Shannon awake at midnight. 'Wake up. It's your birthday dinner.' I follow recipes to the letter even using a stop watch if the timing seems critical. Two minutes is two minutes as far as I'm concerned. Not Charles. Julia Child's instructions for beef bourguignon which I held to be inviolable were violated by Charles's scribbled note in the margin: more onions. We tried James Beard but were forced to cook the stuffed pork chops twice as long as his instructions called for, a delay which turned the green beans into a soggy mass, making Charles happy. A Southern boy, he never appreciated vegetables al dente.

Dinner over, we sank back into a pile of goose-down pillows, Charles still wearing his blue and white striped apron, a last glass of wine next to the large, square, cut-glass ashtray on the coffee table; me curled up, my feet in his lap;

the children silently sneaking off, one by one. Charles would thumb through whatever our current enthusiasm was, find the place where we had left off, give me a few lines in summary in case I had forgotten. Then, he'd start reading. For months it was Henry Steele Commager's *History of America*.

'We are the only people in the world,' he would say, 'who read Commager aloud cover to cover.'

We drifted on. *John Brown's Body*. Archibald MacLeash. Mark Twain. Emily Dickinson.

'You were asleep.'

'No, I wasn't.'

'Yes, you were.'

For Pat at Christmas*

Though I am different from you,
We were born involved in one another.
                                        —Tao Ch'ien

(He meant 'each other' —C.K.)

'What I will give you …'
(A Christmas I.O.U.)

A string of pearls
A suit and sweater
A Rubens print
A holly tree
 And me.

A mixing bowl
A sofa and chair
A set of china
A butcher knife
My life.

*A greeting card containing a Tao Ch'ien quotation, with a grammatical
'correction' by Charles and a message inside.

The Seventies were wrapped in bright sunshine and twinkling lights. We lived it up in marvy Marin where too much was not enough. We would be, Charles said, yuppies, if we weren't so old. Like a painting by Matisse, each nook and cranny in Belvedere and Tiburon was a study in grace. Brilliant parchment flowers on thick bougainvillea vines soared through trees, weaving a line of color as Pete Seeger wove his golden thread through and above and over the voices filling Golden Gate Park. White sails on the blue bay, brown shingled houses in a riot of green, drunken birds reeling from red pyracantha berries, nothing orderly, everything radiant.

Christmas took on a special glow. We went to the Messiah for the first time at the new St. Mary's Cathedral, Mother shifting on the unaccustomed hardness of the wooden pew.

'I'm not going to do that again, Pat. I'm sore.'

She didn't go again, either, not to the Opera House nor to the new Louise Davies Symphony Hall both of which promised a soft cushion. The kids were astonished at the length of Handel's *Messiah*. Rising during the *Hallelujah* chorus, was, J.R. opined, like a seventh-inning stretch.

Charles and I shopped, stopping at the windows of Gump's and Sak's to watch gnomes swinging on diamond necklaces and beautiful ladies alighting from holly-draped sleighs. We put cricks in our necks craning to see the top of the glowing Christmas tree soaring through the Neiman-Marcus rotunda. Swept up in a happy glow we hurried in and out of the Provence boutique with a set of dishes under our arms, pausing briefly to pick up a scarf at a London shop aromatic with the smell of leather, then on to Williams-Sonoma for a maple chopping block so heavy four men had to carry it down the winding steps to the house.

It became a tradition to end the Christmas shopping day at Rene Verdon's La Trianon on O'Farrel Street. Monsieur Verdon cooked for the Kennedy's in the White House, but, like Camelot, La Trianon succumbed to gaudier times. Charles, the Southern gentleman he truly was, I the lady I longed to be, waited expectantly for Madame Verdon to bring us a drink. Charles ordered, grandly gesturing in my direction, 'She will have … ' A feast of subtle French dishes arrived from the kitchen and after the last perfect raspberry had disappeared from under its sheath of creme fraiche, Chef Verdon came by to chat. There has never been a place or a time I liked better.

We spent Christmas week at Tahoe as often as we could, Charles shuttling in and out, spending more time at airports and on airplanes than is good for anyone. He often spent Christmas Eve with his parents on North Carolina's Outer Banks arriving from Charlotte after a Christmas Day crammed with frustrated holiday travelers and delayed aircraft. Sometimes, he arrived home just as the day was drawing to a close. Sometimes, he didn't make it until the next morning. During one holiday season CBS News was taping an ill-starred hour program, a precursor to *60 Minutes*. Charles was flying in and out of San Francisco. I was driving back and forth from the Lake to pick him up. We were both wrecks as attested to by an hilarious picture of the family taken early one morning in front of the Christmas tree. I'm looking comatose in a black robe, Charles is smiling his professional smile, Mother and the children look fairly normal. That picture, in color no less, has been reprinted in newspapers all over the States accompanying stories trying to make sense of our lives. One look at the picture should have ended the discussion. There was no sense in our lives.

There was little sense in the new show either, apparently, or maybe too much sense. I do recall a piece on Leopold Stokowski which may have doomed it with its high-class tone. At any rate the show was dropped after two or three airings. Dan Rather, Barbara Howar and Charles, working hard, had divvied up the three segments, and, as I recall, divided up the anchoring as well. At one point Charles who had just been introduced to Ms. Howar welcomed her to the new show saying he was certain he could learn a lot from her. Ms. Howar, an outspoken Southern belle, writer cum personality with a large past, replied, 'If that's true, Charlie, we're in tough shit.'

No matter how tired he was when he arrived at Tahoe, lopsided with the weight of a bulging bag, one shoulder an inch or two lower than the other, Charles would disappear behind a closed door for an hour or two, frantically tying bows on foil-wrapped packages. He would reappear, pulling from its smudged powder-blue envelope Dylan Thomas' *A Child's Christmas in Wales*, drop onto a sofa and pat the cushion next to him invitingly. The children and their friends would emerge from various corners of the house. Charles would begin to read.

> One Christmas was so much like another,
> in those years around the sea-town corner now
> and out of all sound except the distant speaking
> of the voices I sometimes hear a moment before sleep …

When Charles was away from home, his nightly calls from On The Road were a blueprint to the way he worked. The first night on location, he sketched in the background. On the way to where ever he was, he skimmed through local chronicles, read the newspaper, caught the radio talk shows and already knew as much as the resident historian. He added a wash of color describing untended magnolias heavy with scent; milky hues of peeling paint on an old dory; fields of ripening corn under a scorching sun. The second day he'd have stories. 'And she said,' Charles would launch into a passable imitation, quoting, 'we named it the Bad Penny, because a bad penny always turns up.' The third day Charles would wrap it up, write the piece and read it to me with parenthetical asides on the film footage. By the time the story closed the CBS *Evening News* on Friday night, I was certain I had seen it before.

Charles glided across the television air waves and left behind a dusting of luminous particles as a comet does when it streaks across a star-laden sky. Like a comet, we barely glimpsed him before he was gone. No journey will rival the trail he blazed in television news. This was a time when television was viewed as a great promise, enlarging our lives, before it became a simple commercial venture. Charles gave us pictures of ourselves, not our politicians, not our priests, not our psychoanalysts, but of ourselves. He believed our lives were valuable. He heartened us, and for a moment we thought perhaps he was right. In the early days of On The Road, Charles did what would today take a dozen people to accomplish, directors, producers, editors, writers, researchers, floor assistants, production assistants, secretaries. Charles did it alone. He selected the story. He did the research. With the help of his cameraman, Izzy Bleckman, he planned the camera shots. He did the interviews. He edited the film. He typed out the story on his old Underwood. He both narrated and anchored the piece. He shipped the film and copy off to New York. In the midst of all that movement he created a new style of television reporting. He added to the film; he wrote to the pictures. He was masterful at using silence. Charles' pauses were a reportorial *retarde*, grabbing at your emotions, prodding your intellect. Add to that his voice. The *New York Times* wrote of celebrity journalists spending fortunes on voice teachers while trying to emulate Charles' 'mello cello.' He came by that naturally. It was his great gift.

While not every story was memorable—try as I may I cannot remember the full ten year output—most were better than anything you're likely to see on the evening news at the turn of the century. Many were pure gold. The last run of the Wabash Cannonball. The soft accents of the North Carolina tobacco auctioneer. The aging university professor spending his retirement years sweeping out the gym on his old mid-Western campus. The heroic men who built the

Golden Gate Bridge. The Picking family who spent decades supplying copper kettles to candy makers and snare drums to symphony orchestras. One of their kettles sits beside the fireplace in the Montana cabin. It is an oversized, flat-bottomed kettle which we use for firewood. A small plaque on the side gives its maker's name: Mr. Robert Picking, Bucyrus, Ohio. Mr. Picking was an old man when Charles did the story on the family business, and showed an old man's pride in his craft. Our kettle is so well made it will turn up in some archeological dig in the next millennium giving pause to academics who will wonder what was going on here at the edge of the Big Hole River a thousand years ago.

One story, a day in the life of a garbage collector in Napa Valley, led to my presenting Charles a baseball signed by one of his heroes, Joe DiMaggio, a man private and diffident not unlike Charles himself. The man who put Charles onto the loquacious garbage collector was Tom Rooney, a San Francisco public relations guru. Mr. Rooney drank with Mr. DiMaggio in his bar in the City, a custom envied by Charles who was too reticent to request an introduction. For Charles' birthday one year I asked Mr. Rooney to ask Mr. Di Maggio for an autographed baseball. Mr. Rooney good-naturedly agreed and suggested I come by the bar one early afternoon to pick it up. I arrived in a paroxysm of fear, feeling like a gawky rustic, blushing and bumping into empty stools before reaching the trio of men which included Mr. DiMaggio casually watching my advance. Joe DiMaggio, I kept thinking. Charles' hero. A macho Italian type who surely laughed at feminist fumblings. Joe DiMaggio who married Marilyn Monroe. The graceful god of baseball who when Marilyn said to him, 'Joe, you have never heard such cheering,' coolly replied, 'Yes, I have.' I grabbed the proffered baseball and fled. 'How about them Yankees?' Charles crowed caressing the ball. I felt I had scored a home run myself.

Charles' bicentennial series, On The Road to '76, gave us trenchant sketches, Leonardo on film, of what we are about in this country. In Montana he visited the site of Custer's last stand. In a few quick strokes he painted the battle, the Pyrrhic victory leading inexorably to the brutal massacre at Wounded Knee. Gray, silent windmills marked the passing of the unfenced Great Plains in Nebraska. He ended the fifty-week series with a fifteen-minute summary at Philadelphia's Liberty Hall, quoting each delegate, Benjamin Franklin, John Adams, Mr. Carroll of Carrollton, Charles' voice arguing, pleading, explaining the debate on the Declaration of Independence, tallying the vote as men pledged their lives, their fortunes and their sacred honor. On the day of our nation's 200th birthday party Charles was stationed aboard a Coast Guard vessel in New York harbor covering the parade of Tall Ships. I was stationed on our front deck covering the reprise of all fifty-one On The Road to '76 stories.

I watched just about every On The Road segment. Sometimes it required a little effort. I was in downtown Reno when the story of Teddy Roosevelt's dedication to our national parks was scheduled to run. Elbowing my way up the escalator to Harold's Club second floor bar I cajoled the bartender to change the channel, and while toying with a Coke over chippie ice managed to catch the last five minutes of the evening news. Driving down Highway 101 through Eureka, California one summer, Charles in a moment of desperation rented a motel room for the Friday night story, which, I am embarrassed to say, I have forgotten.

The On The Road crew, Izzy Bleckman, Charlie Quinlan and Larry Gianneschi, worked an average of two weeks at a stretch. An easy life. Those guys have it made, Charles would mutter enviously. He, on the other hand, worked just about everyday, writing when he was home, running down fluorescent-lit corridors, clutching his bag, to catch a plane when he was away, hailing taxis, checking in and out of hotels, collapsing after a long day with a steak and a beer in his room. Charles gave liberal speeches to conservative corporations for a fee, spoke free of charge to university classes, lent his prestige to folk festivals and the occasional museum opening as a way of paying his dues. He let himself be dragooned into flashy CBS network entertainments for CBS affiliates, dropped in on local CBS station managers and news directors, buying them lunch, boosting their morale. He gave interviews on the radio, to newspaper reporters, on local television stations, to magazine writers, it didn't matter, he rarely said no. Charles justified this time I thought not only wasted but draining, by patiently, and sometimes impatiently, explaining to me that he made his living as a reporter interviewing others; he had an obligation to those other reporters who requested interviews of him.

Charles' books, whether collections of his television and radio pieces or new work, all demanded full-scale promotional schedules, talk shows, local and national, book signings, cocktail parties. When he sprinted into his New York office to see what was going on at headquarters, voluminous quantities of mail greeted him. Reams of paper would pile up week after week until in despair he would pick out a few letters to answer and sweep the rest into a waste basket or onto his unfortunate secretary's desk. Struggling writers were always after him for a recommendation, an introduction, advice or just a few kind words. If a work struck his fancy, Charles tapped out a paragraph or two assuring the would-be author a publisher. At the bottom of the seemingly endless list loomed the bottomless hole of the expense account, an immense maw, demanding, never satisfied. Charles would fall months, years behind on his expenses. Threats would come down from Black Rock, the CBS New York headquarters. Charles would fume, ignoring them as long as he could. At one point a CBS accountant refused him any more advances until he came within hailing distance of the current year. Charles was reduced to borrowing morning coffee money from Charlie Quinlan before finally settling down to the task.

Once a week Charles squeezed an hour or two out of his schedule to write a radio piece. Many, maybe all, CBS News correspondents were expected to provide fodder for a weekly series. Charles's show was Dateline America. Never taken seriously by anyone but the producer, the three or four minute narrative was heard once a week over the CBS radio network. Charles dashed it off, typing as fast as he could and recorded it without giving it much thought. Sometimes it was a spin-off of that week's On The Road story. More often it was Charles letting off steam on whatever irked or amused him as he charted the country's progress on America's back roads. As every writer, journalist and academic knows, one can always pick up a little extra cash effortlessly by bundling a collection of scraps of paper—speeches, columns, letters, random thoughts jotted down on the back of napkins—slapping them between two hard covers, and calling it a book. *Dateline America*, a collection of eighty-four scripts, appeared in 1979 bringing with it the eagerly awaited windfall of a royalty check. 'We're rich,' Charles said, feeling, if possible, more pleased than usual with the world.

Dateline America reveals the inner Charles in a way nothing else he did even comes close to. That includes his disarming *A Life on the Road*. *Dateline America* is a bit acerbic, often very funny and can be used as a scorecard of late twentieth century foibles as we stumbled toward our brave new world. Charles bemoaned the loss of real food. 'They are making gravy out of chemicals. They call it old-style country gravy. They are making bacon out of soybeans. They are mixing seaweed and gelatin and calling it pineapple.' He gave tips to travelers: 'If you don't like loud rock music, change the settings on the rental car radio as soon as you rent it. The guys who park rental cars all like rock music, and the push buttons of all rental car radios are set for rock stations. Sometimes *all* the buttons are set for the *same* rock station.' He erupted when words were used to mean just the opposite of what they said. 'For Your Convenience,' we are substituting hot air for hand towels. 'For Your Protection,' we no longer accept cash for room payment. This docilely accepted business demand sent Charles into an inner rage. Arriving at a generic motel late one evening and being met with the demand for a credit card plus identification laminated on assorted IDs, Charles listed the thousands of dollars worth of equipment he was leaving in the motel's parking lot and demanded proof of the staff's lack of criminal intent. He could be fierce when aroused. If I feel in danger of losing Charles, it is *Dateline America* I reach for.

My own labors during those years, not to put too fine a point on it, stumbled along somewhere between dilettantism and self-indulgence. No longer galvanized by a stack of overdue bills, I stopped looking for a job that would pay fifty dollars more a month than the one I currently held. I started looking for excitement. I quit the Labor Department.

Feminism catapulted me into a new career.

Charles flew in one afternoon bravely carrying the first issue of *MS Magazine* concealed within the covers of *New York*. Our household, already writhing with feminist quirks, became a war zone as Charles and I brawled over the *I Want a Wife* essay until the next issue of *MS* replaced it with the *I Want a Husband* rebuttal. When *Against Our Will* hit the bookstalls, we carried on the argument during nightly phone calls, Charles hanging up in a fury, calling back, hanging up again. On a fishing trip at Convict Lake, California, we argued so loudly over dinner, the next night Charles, chagrined, handed out tips to the staff before we even ordered our meal. On a particularly rousing evening in our Belvedere dining room which jutted out over a jasmine scented garden, a discussion of whether or not Greek civilization was worthy of emulation hinged on the Hellenic belief that women were inferior. The argument deteriorated to the point that Charles, no longer able to contain himself, jumped up and slammed the French doors so vehemently a pane of glass broke. The next morning, before we crept out of bed shame-faced, J.R. had the door off, the shattered pane replaced and the door back on, enabling us to ignore the whole affair, at least, until after breakfast.

These clashes were so exhilarating that I set up a one-woman rabble-rousing shop, Pat Shannon Baker and Associates. Charles advised me to put in commas and bring in the troops: Pat, Shannon, Baker (J.R.), and Associates (Kathleen). The troops weren't interested. I left the Feds with only one success, a slide show with voice over using Judy Dater's ground-breaking photos of women and Charles narrating quotes from John Stuart Mill's *On The Subjection of Women.*

In my new incarnation I set about giving speeches, lectures, seminars, quoting endlessly from Mary Wollstonecraft and Virginia Woolf even as Charles pointed out that nobody gave a damn about Mary Wollstonecraft. He was right, as usual. My careful chronicles got me shouldered aside by laid-back types who attributed the world's problems to a lack of centering. These self-styled gurus made me grit my teeth as audiences fell into a kind of collective trance lulled by hypnotic new-age jargon.

The *Milwaukee Journal* summed up my adventures in a lead paragraph. 'A self-professed feminist stood up before what has been called a conservative nurses group Wednesday night and said, "Give me liberty or give me death." There was an awkward silence.'

That was Victoria Woodhull, of course, at the 1872 suffrage convention in New York City. 'We mean treason; we mean secession, and on a thousand times grander scale than was that of the South. We are plotting revolution; we will overthrow this bogus Republic and plant a government of righteousness in its stead … '

The start of what might have been a useful life faltered as night after night I went AWOL. Impassioned women, ready to breach the ramparts, looked around and found me missing during the all-night strategy sessions that inevitably followed a rousing call to arms. I had deserted them, slinking into the nearest cab to spend a voluptuous night with Charles savoring blinis, smothered in sour cream and Beluga caviar, washed down with a heady cabernet and only a hint of guilt.

DATELINE AMERICA

CHICAGO. A guy in a bar was telling me about the magician in Seattle who predicted the New York power blackout.

'I heard about it,' I said. 'I don't believe it.'

'You don't *believe* it?' he said. 'It was a fact.'

'It was a trick,' I said.

'I can't believe you don't believe it,' he said.

'Believe it,' I said. 'You want to know what else I don't believe?'

I said. 'I don't believe in the Loch Ness Monster. I don't believe in the Bermuda Triangle. I think the Abominable Snowman is an abominable publicity stunt to promote tourism in Nepal.'

'What about Big Foot?' the guy asked.

'Big Foot is a big put-on,' I said. 'So are UFO's. They always turn out to be swamp gas or the Goodyear Blimp.'

'Yeah?' the guy said. 'What about the UFO that landed in Pascagoula, Mississippi, a few summers ago and gave those two fishermen a ride?'

'Look,' I said, 'if there are beings on another planet intelligent enough to send a spaceship to earth, they are also intelligent enough not to land in Pascagoula, Mississippi, in the summertime.'

The argument was getting loud and people started staring.

'What's your birth sign?' somebody asked.

'Virgo,' I said.

'Virgos are skeptical,' he said.

'I said, "I do not believe in astrology." Everybody looked appalled.'

Somebody asked, 'You don't believe in the Age of Aquarius?'

'I believe in the Age of Enlightenment,' I said, 'and we need one in this bar.'

People started murmuring incredulously and pointing fingers at me, and I decided to let them have it.

'I don't believe in alpha waves,' I said. 'I don't believe in gurus from India or ancient astronauts from Venus. I don't believe in the Lost Dutchman gold mine or the Lost City of Atlantis. I don't believe in biorhythms. I don't believe in psychoanalysis. I don't believe in Marxism or mermaids or playing Mozart to houseplants."

'Far out!' the first guy said. 'What do you believe?'

I considered the question. 'I believe,' I said, 'that the Cubs have a chance to win the pennant.'

The guy groaned. 'Oh, man,' he said. 'If you believe that, you'll believe anything.'

Charles Kuralt

There is a breed of men who cannot stay still. Some lead successful lives. For some defeat lies at the end of the quest. Charles worked with a singular vigor and was rewarded with a laurel wreath. Prey to restless discontent, Daddy's lot fell to the latter. Living with these two nomads, first the one and then the other, granted me a way of looking at things that is foreign to those whose perspective is limited to a fixed position. My true inheritance from both men is the view of the outsider.

As Leslie Fiedler scathingly pointed out in his appraisal of the Montana face, growing up in the western United States in the Thirties and Forties one rarely encountered a Negro or a servant or a Jew. That didn't mean we were locked into a static culture. Though it might look so to an Easterner, the West was not a monolith. Potsherds of myriad civilizations littered the landscape. When one is always on the move the way we were, you don't have time to check out the bona fides; like a lost puppy you just nuzzle up to whoever puts out a bowl of warm milk. This might be the banker's daughter, but it could just as easily be the lonely Armenian refugee wracked by scenes of Turkish cruelties. Unless you were blinded like poor Gloucester, it was impossible to escape the silent stares of dispossessed Indians some of whom had themselves escaped from our own massacres of the late 1800s. In my world eccentrics jousted with the narrow-minded. Outcasts broke the tedium of small town life. Ethnics prodded parochial politics into lively new territories, and the West's spiritual domain was festooned with an array of fluttering banners. Fourth generation Mormons jostled just-arrived Basque Catholics, and Jehovah's Witnesses vied with Seventh Day Adventists. Dogmatism dies a sudden death when it is in constant collision with new ideas.

My father and Charles, so different in so many ways, shared a devout humanism. I hold a lifetime membership in that club though I struggle to match their tolerance. My personal chapter of Pat Robertson's derided secular humanists leans more to the morose and the melancholy than theirs did, an inclination which gave both Daddy and Charles considerable pain and irritation. The two men also shared an unblinkered view of life's absurdities which gave bite to their personalities. Even-tempered, entertained and diverted by man's frailties, they could be crotchety and were hard put to bear fools lightly. When Daddy, whom I loved as I loved Charles, died in March of 1973 it was Charles who squeezed my hand, pleading, 'Please don't cry like this when I die.' Impossible advice for a sackcloth and ashes person like me.

Charles and I attended a sparkling performance of *A Midsummer Night's Dream* by the touring Royal Shakespeare Company at San Francisco's Geary Theater and were sleeping contentedly when the telephone rang at six in the morning. It was Mother.

'Jack is dead.'

Not dead, but dying. Charles and I flew to Reno, to Mother waiting for us, waiting for Daddy to die. Doctors and nurses and patients knew we would soon be there. Daddy, conscious and garrulous, sang out his mantra.

'My daughter is coming; she is coming from San Francisco; she is coming.'

My sister Roberta's husband, in Reno on Forest Service business, took Daddy out to celebrate St. Patrick's Day. They were home early. Daddy was cheerful. The night uneventful. Without warning his heart stopped. Roberta drove down from Wells. Like families the world over, we sat and held hands, sad and impotent. Before Charles flew out on Monday morning to point the wandering On The Road crew in a direction, he bought skeins of heavy wool, unbleached, and picked out an intricate Irish afghan pattern from the notions department in the old Gray Reid's Department Store. 'Knit this,' he said. I did. The thick, sculpted coils earn their keep these nights warding off the damp Derrynavglaun winter.

Daddy died on Tuesday morning never leaving intensive care. I wept, I love you, Daddy, bending over him, stroking his forehead. He didn't go quietly. Minutes before he died he pushed a bowl of jello out of a young nurse's hand onto the floor, irate at an equally young doctor, smiling, as he assured us all would be well. Daddy was not about to be hood-winked at that late date.

We took him back to his birthplace, to Ravenna's Mt. Calvary. It was to be a homecoming, but it turned bitter. Too many years had flown by since Daddy had set foot on Nebraska soil. There was only one grave site left in our family plot. It was destined to be Mary's, Daddy's sister, who stayed behind assuming the burdens that were rightfully his when he so casually strolled out of their lives. The small, crumbling town long ago decided who would be buried next to Clara and John Andrew, his and Mary's mother and father, but I would not have it. Charles laughed gloomily, when he met us there, shaking his head. I was, he said, a raging Antigone searching for a place to bury her dead. Charles made peace with the town's attorney whom I had enraged, and the minister, and the startled people at the undertakers, Love and Rhode. He walked the still-frozen ground under the leafless trees with the townspeople, checking again the burial plot register neatly penned by a century of town clerks, finding, at last, an unmarked grave in our plot of a long ago still-born child lying beside Maren and Thomas Larkin, my great-grandmother and great-grandfather. Here, it was agreed, Daddy could at last lie down with his family to rest.

Daddy's last present to me was a red rose candle held upright on a wrought iron stem, a spray of leaves cradling his message. 'Only a rose for you today. JS Happy birthday, Pat.'

His loss left me crumpled.

After years of aimless drinking and a string of auto repair shops, Daddy snatched a second wind when he turned seventy and turned sober. The two years before his death were a blur of activity, manic after years of depression. The last metal door opening into a cold, concrete cubicle—its walls a fantastic display of hanging tools, each wiped clean, each in its proper place, hot air fan dangling from the ceiling, windows blurred by rising mists of lacquer—was padlocked shut. As the hope of a big strike disappeared with the veins of ore petering out under the Western desert, Daddy finally reconciled himself to the end of a dream. He began to see advantages in being a tin-beater. On retiring the first thing he did was write an essay about the arcane practices of a body shop:

> The author of this little book has spent thirty years of almost constant association with the autobody repair business … its rewards are particularly attractive to the rugged individuals who place freedom of action above all else.

He liked writing and became convinced he could make money peddling yarns. He went to the local newsstand and picked up magazines aimed at the hopeful hack. He set up his own clipping service, pasting whatever caught his fancy into a cloth covered ledger. He searched for markets, found some, invested $129.40 in a Smith Corona portable and started churning out boiler plate. Acknowledging his lack of typing skills, he browbeat Mother into becoming his editorial assistant. She was alternately bemused and vexed by the appointment.

'Damn it, Jack, I can't to this,' she wailed. 'Do it yourself.'

Undeterred, he relentlessly pointed out typing errors and misspelled words, raising stock prices on correcto tape and white-out liquid. Mother labored on, cursing and complaining, pounding the cranky portable with two arthritic fingers, a slither of onion skins growing over the months into a sizable stack. These she filed under two categories, submission and rejection.

When Charles and I bought Shannon a puppy, Able Baker, for her birthday, Daddy's indignation at our cavalier treatment of the little Sheltie prompted him to take us to task:

> The author intends that the following paragraphs in no way be applied to the knowledgeable adult … (but) a little thoughtful planning should take place in a home about to acquire a pet for a school age child.

On the new puppy's arrival, Charles christened him Able Baker Charlie Dog. Late in life Able Baker was mournfully re-christened Disabled Baker after suffering a collision with a speeding car.

Daddy's new career as a writer couldn't begin to use up his energies. He bought a used bicycle.

'Jack,' Mother blustered, 'you're gonna' kill yourself.'

After she insisted she would never again clean and bandage his bleeding shins, he sought help in another direction, sending off to the Athletic Institute for an *Improve Your Cycling* pamphlet. He bought a Ruger Blackhawk .357 pistol and took out a membership in the Silver State Rifle and Pistol Club, driving out to the range twice a week in the old Buick for target practice. In his ramblings he came across a used Leica, $10 down, $10 a month, and snapped roll after roll of out-of-focus shots of the ducks and geese pillaging Virginia Lake.

He was rushing toward the end. He didn't get a chance to plant his Morning Glory seeds beneath the front window. We all leave things undone. Twenty years later Charles' father was waiting delivery of two Clematis plants, the dark purple jackmanii and the new cultivar, niobe, when death overtook him. Charles sent the two dry-looking twigs on to me at Derrynavglaun. There they struggle to survive along with the Clematis montana 'Alba' and montana 'Rubins' which Charles and I planted above the rock wall behind the kitchen our first year at Derrynavglaun.

Daddy left his own epitaph in a book of poetry he gave Mother before he died.

Life is a journey and not a home; a road, not a city of habitation …

After burying Daddy in his family's plot back in Nebraska, Mother, exhausted and full of grief, lay on the bed, weeping.

'Everyone wanted the Gold Man,' she told Charles, 'but I got him.'

It was a Faustian bargain.

The scraps of Daddy's life could be pieced into a colorful crazy quilt. Sepia-toned photographs and spidery handwriting marked the trail West. With Mother it was a different story. Charles learned more about Mother's life than we ever knew as he stayed with her through the long night listening to her memories. Bits of her past he shared with us. The rest he kept to himself.

When my sister and I were growing up there seemed nothing substantial to hang onto relative to Mother's early life. Roberta and I would forget what we had said the last time we had been asked to give an account of ourselves. Maiden names and birth dates, ethnic origins and place of birth, were always a problem. As a babe, Mother had been cast into the wilderness by unforgiving Baptist righteousness. She emerged from her lonely wanderings, a young woman, eyes narrowed in distrusting, unflinching gaze. The first thing she saw that day in Boulder, Colorado was Jack Shannon, the Gold Man. That is the first time we see her. For all we know she sprang whole from the head of Zeus. Wanda might have been a Nelson. Or, maybe a Jackson? Perhaps, she lived in Texas, but why not Oklahoma?

Had there been a reservation with silent Cherokees or a boom town with boisterous wild-catters? She rode in covered wagons. She made lye in an outside tub to wash a farmer's clothes. At revival meetings she drew herself into the tiniest, hardest, most unreachable place and would not, no matter the threats of damnation, repent. The one fact we are certain of is the cruelest. She was unwanted, tossed from family to family.

She stands before us, defiant, a band across her forehead, a plain cotton frock concealing a tiny figure. Years later an old friend would take delight in hectoring her; ninety pounds of burnt powder, he would chortle. She cared for the Western *nouveau riche* and their children, but it was she who must have been a handful. There was nothing humble or obsequious in her demeanor. Mother had a streak as unforgiving and as unrelenting as the Baptist preachers. Brow-beat parents must have sighed with relief when she went on her way.

Mother freed herself from the suffocating isolation of a servant's life when she reached Boulder hurtling into the boisterous *laissez-faire* of a raw, working class cafe. Not easy, slinging hash, but you gave as good as you got. She rouged her knees and chain-smoked, tossing her sleekly bobbed hair over untouched glasses of bootleg gin. The twanging lyrics of 'Red River Valley' seeped through the baritone of a guitar as the Gold Man sang to her. She stayed ferociously loyal to him for over forty years. Now, her Gold Man was gone.

Mother moved to Wells to be close to Roberta. It was a good place for her.

'I love this good old desert,' she explained to Charles when I became too pushy about dragging her to Marin County.

She lived alone, visiting the fog-shrouded Bay Area, but scurrying back to the sagebrush sooner rather than later. Hoeing, raking, planting, she grew tomatoes and green onions and radishes, sending care packages to Charles and me in California. Cookouts and fishing trips in the Ruby Mountains found her at day's end lounging beside a glowing campfire with a can of beer in one hand, a cigarette in the other, surrounded by pick-up trucks, Stetson hats, dogs and tents.

Ireland, when I first visited over twenty years ago, was a poor country locked into two myths. The first was of a romantic bawneen-clad Celt warrior half-hidden in thousand-year-old mists. The second, equally romantic but far more dangerous fable, told of the exploits of the hard men of the Irish Republican Army who at that time could be spotted on back roads wearing the ubiquitous balaclava-and-rifle attire favored by guerrillas the world over. Both the Celtic warriors and the IRA hardliners managed to wreck more havoc on their brothers and Eire than they ever did on their sworn nemesis, the Brits. In-fighting is a high art among the Irish. Irish writer Brendan Behan summed it up, ' … if we're Republicans we've got to have a split.' Violence is not my cup of tea, but independent thought is. On my first trip to the Emerald Isle if I caught a political discussion at the local pub, there were likely to be as many opinions as Irishmen in the room. None was a parroting of the night's television news. In the Seventies Ireland was a poor country in monetary terms, but it was rich in talk and ideas.

The European Union changed the equation pouring in billions of dollars until Ireland today has the fastest growing economy in Europe. Where before men slung knife-edged slanes over their shoulder before striding off to the bog to cut a winter's supply of turf, their kids, boys and girls alike, are more likely seated in front of a computer screen. The advantages of a middle-class life are obvious. Warm, dry homes. Good education. Well-paying jobs. No back-breaking labor. The easily paid price is a certain conformity of thought. Pub talk is now a direct steal from well-groomed news readers. When I complained about the change to an old friend, Johnny Casey, he told me a story. It was of his father exulting the first time he clamped an outboard engine onto his curragh, the heavy, dependable craft Conamara men use for fishing. 'Now, I can sail into the wind.' Johnny said the old days only look good to people like me who didn't have to live in them.

That first trip to Ireland was a Christmas present, a gift from Charles to salve my injured feelings. All three of the kids had been to Europe. Charles had been all over the world. In our ten years together, the only place I had been outside the lower forty-eight was Baja. That didn't hardly count. I wanted to go to Ireland, because I thought I was Irish. One of Daddy's favorite reminiscences was of his little Scotch-Irish grandmother feeding hungry remnants of the Pawnee tribes from the back porch of the Halsey ranch in western Nebraska. It wasn't until I was actually in Northern Ireland that I came to realize Scotch-Irish did not mean half Scotch and half Irish. It meant being a descendent of the Scottish plantation people who were lured into the North by the British Crown in an effort to stifle Irish claims to sovereignty. That was back in the 1600s. It worked, sort of. The northern six counties remain a part of the UK, but as any American who has a nodding acquaintance with the news knows, the battle goes on stymieing the peace the majority of the island people long for.

If my view of Irish history had been a little less muddled, I might have picked up on an obvious clue in my family background. The Larkins and Hutchinsons and Shannons were all Protestant, Scottish Celts. Irish Celts are Roman Catholic. As an American I was surprised to discover Irish institutions, both in the North and in the Republic, are strongly sectarian. These segregated schools do little to defuse an already tense situation in the North. Some Americans feel the separation of church and state is an onerous burden and urge prayer in public school. They might do us a favor reading of the bloodshed Ireland has been subjected to by the stress in public schools on religious differences. Yet, on a social basis, the Irish do not give a damn what religion you are. Individually, they are an extraordinarily tolerant people. Ireland is a most perfect place to begin an understanding of the world.

Charles was swathed in religious tolerance despite the fact that he himself lacked religious fervor. Once asked if he was a Christian, he replied, 'More or less,' to which his questioner replied, 'More is better.' I become exercised over religious questions and can spend hours decrying pious excesses. Charles was an agnostic uninterested in the pros and cons of belief unless those beliefs inhibited the beliefs of others. My litanies of sectarian malfeasance bored Charles. 'Charles, religion is responsible for all the conflict in the world. Look around.' Charles would roll his eyes and try to change the subject. He wasn't interested in theological debate. He was interested in issues which could be attacked and solved by the human intellect.

One of Charles' heroes was Thomas Jefferson. Charles would quote John Kennedy's remark to a dinner party of

Nobel Laureates held at the White House. There is more talent in this room tonight than at any time since Thomas Jefferson sat down to dinner alone. Early on in our lives together, Charles took me on a Jefferson tour. It began with a reading of the first volume of Dumas Malone's biography on our third, and in Charles' mind, greatest president, leaving me a comfortable stack of volumes for bedtime perusal in his absence. After I finished my reading, the Jefferson tour moved to the Hay-Adams Hotel in Washington D.C. where we sat gazing out of our window scrutinizing the lighted rooms in the White House wishing it was Mr. Jefferson and not Mr. Nixon who would sleep there that night.

From D.C. we drove south to Virginia and walked the wide, winding path to Monticello, listening for the hoof beats of Mr. Jefferson's horse, the sound of the President returning home from the Capital. Here, Charles read Jefferson's thoughts on religious freedom: ' … the impious presumption of legislators and rulers, civil as well as ecclesiastical, who, being themselves but fallible and uninspired men, have assumed dominion over the faith of others, setting up their own opinions and modes of thinking as the only true and infallible, and as such endeavoring to impose them on others, hath established and maintained false religions over the greatest part of the world and through all time … ' After Charles' tour I was well-equipped to corner beleaguered Dublin booksellers, advancing arguments in favor of a shelf on Jefferson—of whom they had nary a book—as a small counterbalance to the bulging shelves crammed with the pithy writings of Irish saints and sinners.

Charles booked a room for me at the Shelbourne Hotel where the gentry stood by the windows disdainfully viewing the 1916 Easter Uprising, the opening skirmish in a war that led to Irish independence. The treads on the grand staircase creak with age and the overstuffed sofas in the lounge invite lingering. It is the most splendid hotel in Dublin not because of the old turf fire which has recently been replaced by a gas burner but because Thackery stayed there in the 1840s when he toured Ireland unknowingly chronicling the early days of the Famine. The Shelbourne sits on the edge of St. Stephen's Green, an easy stroll either to the Book of Kells lying in state at Trinity College or over to Bewley's on Grafton Street for a cup of coffee thick with cream.

Still in my brashest feminist phase, I immediately collided with Old World custom by leaving sturdy walking shoes outside the door of my room for polishing as suggested in the hotel's list of offerings. The next morning I found a note stuffed into one grimy toe informing me only gentlemen's shoes were accepted for the nightly rub-down. It probably hadn't helped that I carried only a backpack stuffed with tweed knickers and knee-high woolen socks when I checked into this genteel establishment, but the American habit of over-tipping softened, somewhat, the look of disdain on the face of the concierge.

I had a plan for my six week stay. It was to bed down in farmhouse accommodations and interview farm wives, find out how the feminist revolution changed their lives. After a night or two of Dublin luxury I eased into the driver's seat of a rental car as the Shelbourne doorman whispered helpful hints for driving on the left side of the road. With a map of Ireland open on the seat beside me, a guide to farmhouse accommodations tucked in a side pocket and a coin purse bursting with five and ten pence pieces for telephone change, I headed into the countryside. It was February. Nothing is open in rural Ireland in February. In County Mayo one farmwife took pity on me, it being dark and me being miles from any hotel, and let me stay the night. The next morning, pushing aside good manners, I edged my way into Bridie's kitchen. Bridie had eleven children, one on her hip and one entering the seminary at Maynooth. I asked her if the women's movement had changed her life in any dramatic way. No, she didn't think so. They bought their first car the year before which meant she was able to attend christenings and funerals instead of being homebound all the time. That, she said, was a major change. Technology: One. Feminism: Zero.

I did meet a group of feminists in Dublin attending the first Irishwoman's conference to be held under government sponsorship. The stars of the show were an Irish newspaper reporter and her gang of cohorts. They one-upped the meeting by traveling on a train from Belfast to Dublin throwing out handfuls of condoms at each stop. It was a protest against the Irish law that forbade the dispensing of contraceptives without a doctor's prescription. Charles gave me a little Pentax camera for the trip. With no secret service in sight, I scrambled up on the conference stage and clicked away. I have a close-up of the Ireland's future prime minister, Taoiseach Charles Haughey, affable and dapper, giving his welcoming speech. It reminded me of the days with Paul Laxalt in Nevada when democracy still had that lovely rough and tumble feel.

For six weeks I roamed over Ireland, enraptured by its beauty. In the end it was rocky, barren Conamara in the western most part of the island that entangled me in her strange web. Yellow gorse and purple heather. Lakes without number. Burnished sea weed washed up on sandy beaches. Emptiness.

28 March 78

Dear Mother, I drove the Sky road from Clifden to Letterfrack ... the most breathtaking in Ireland, limestone mountains, jigsaw puzzle coast. There is snow on the Connemara [*sic*] peaks and occasional hail down here ... Love Pat.

Years later wild Conamara became a refuge for me. On this trip seclusion was the last thing on my mind. I wanted to be in the thick of things. While I was traipsing around the Irish coast free as the dark, fast skuas flying in from the North Atlantic for a quick meal of mackeral, Charles and Mother took over the responsibilities back in Belvedere. My call from County Kerry on Easter Sunday interrupted Charles as he carved the pineapple and brown sugar glazed ham while Mother ladled out sweet potatoes topped with marshmallows. They were having a perfectly grand time without me.

The exhilaration of Ireland followed me back to the States. Life was so good even Charles' colostomy didn't seem such a terrible thing. There was a hint of the hypochondriac in his nature, but when he was truly sick, Charles became nonchalant. He quoted Eric Sevareid, 'Even hypochondriacs get sick.' He purposely misled me about the seriousness of illnesses. The day of the operation, he had already telephoned, still groggy from the anesthetic, when his doctor rang to tell me Charles was doing just fine. He was amused to hear Charles and I had already spoken. I bought a linen suit like the one Sydney Greenstreet wore in *Casablanca* and flew to New York, lunching at the Russian Tea Room between visits to New York City–Cornell University Hospital where we paraded up and down the hall, Charles pushing the metal IV stand ahead of him. It was just another adventure.

A year or so before that first trip to Ireland Petie Baird fell ill. I remember the moment Charles told me about her hospitalization. It was Opening Day on San Francisco Bay. There was a chill, April breeze. A friend from my Reno days, Faith Greaves, was visiting. We sat on the deck, wrapped in shawls admiring the parade of brightly-colored mizens, listening to the sounds of jazz wafting up the hill from a neighbor's party. Charles arrived from somewhere on the road mid-afternoon. He rented a car for the drive home so I could spend the day with Faith. He arrived pale and restive, impatient, brusque. Our street was blocked off by visitors' cars. Forced to park on the road above, he slipped on the pavement of the ridiculously steep hill leading down to us. I never saw him as irritable. Faith's car was pulling out of the driveway when Charles turned to me and told me the bad news.

Petie Baird was, I believe, a gallant patient. On-going treatment required repeated hospital stays during the twenty years preceding her death in 1999. She bounced back, attended Broadway openings, traveled with friends, read through the night. I sympathized with her as one does with a distant member of an extended family not realizing a single die had been cast for all of us. If there had ever been plans for a divorce, they were discarded that day.

It wasn't Petie Baird though who kept me unbalanced during those years. It was Clio. Charles's Muse. Charles was a bard, a troubadour, a teller of stories, a singer of songs. As his audience swelled, he left off his wanderings and took up residence in a baronial hall. I could see him smiling, waving, a long way off, a horde of people surrounding him, as a baroque trumpet signaled the rising sun of *Sunday Morning*, the CBS news hour Charles made his own. He charmed America with its own portrait on Sunday mornings. He took us to our museums. Played our music. Examined our politics. Unwrapped the gifts we gave to ourselves, our parks, our forests, our seacoasts. Memorialized the best of us. Gave us what no else could give us. Yet to me the show was a betrayal. It meant Charles was in New York each Saturday and Sunday.

To make matters worse there was a brief period when he was seduced into anchoring the faltering *CBS Morning News*. In an effort to halt a slide in the ratings, CBS showcased a series of correspondents including one of Charles' best friends, Hughes Rudd. An iconoclastic newsman of the old breed, Rudd should have piled up the rating points. It says more about the television audience than it does about Rudd that his efforts failed. Charles was CBS's last ditch effort to keep hard news on the air in the morning hours. I'd get up early, grind coffee, squeeze orange juice, heat the croissant I baked the day before and settle down on the sofa waiting for Charles to tell me what was going on in the world. One morning I turned on the set and saw a glamorous blond in a scarlet dress sitting triumphantly next to the portly man with the subdued paisley handkerchief barely peeping out of his breast pocket. It was Diane Sawyer, an ex-beauty queen, ready to make her mark in television. Her appearance sounded the death knell of the *CBS Morning News* as CBS began dismantling the firewall between hard news and entertainment.

In an uncharacteristically frantic moment Charles suggested we move to Connecticut. On reflection it was a good idea. It would have forced us to face a situation which we did our best to ignore. I wasn't up to it and choose, instead, the coward's path. I closed up the house. Put everything into storage. Went back to Ireland. Flying into Shannon I drove up to Rathmullan in County Donegal on the Northern border. There in the high-ceilinged rooms of a converted country house I talked and walked with shell-shocked Protestants and Catholics stealing a moment of repose from the killings and bombings in the Six Counties. One couple, a gentle historian and his devoted wife of sixty years, owed their allegiance to the Queen, but, nonetheless, took great care to explain the historical imperatives on both sides of the Troubles. It was after the pair returned to Belfast that I learned the old man's brother, a judge, was killed by the IRA. I owe the burial of my certainties about Ireland and the birth of the ambivalence that always accompanies the graying of blacks and whites to those quiet, thoughtful talks.

I meant to stay in Ireland forever, but after six months immersed in the excitement of a new culture, I discovered something. I was a Yank, and I was lonely. I came back to the States at Christmas. We celebrated at Tahoe. Roberta and Harvey and their kids and their kid's kids came to feed the Canada Geese and watch the sun set from the long wooden pier. Eight-year-old Jason pumped frantically as he swung higher and further out over the icy lake waters. We all yelled, 'Go, Jason.' And, beneath the tumult the tiny feminist cry of three-year old Della Marie was all but drowned out, 'Go, Della Marie.' Mother walked the beach picking up colored glass for Charles who assembled a portrait of me in my Irish scarf and cap on a glass-topped bamboo table. We played Scrabble and gin and fictionary. Charles baked a carrot cake in a pan too small for the recipe, and it flowed out of the oven and over the floor. He threw a laughing J.R. out of the kitchen in disgust as the rest of us rushed to clean up the mess. Life was back to normal.

They went by so fast, those years. Kathleen left for Holland and came back plump from eating thick slabs of bread coated with chocolate. She was wasp-waisted the next time we looked as she opened satin-ribboned gifts by a splashing fountain on her twenty-first birthday. In a twinkling of an eye, her thick brown hair softly wind-blown above delicate white lace, she and Dan Stephan walked hand in hand down a soft dirt path to the minister standing at its end. Charles and I watched, thought of our own young marriages, and wondered.

We gave Kathleen a tennis outfit and tennis lessons. We agonized at her struggles. What does it mean to be a woman? Anne Stein's nascent sisterhood, Women On the Move, helped Kathleen sort it out. Gloria Steinem came to speak. Standing at the back of the hall, I couldn't see anything. I could hardly hear. Rising on tip-toe, dodging from side to side, I asked Anne, who is introducing Gloria? Kathleen, she said. Anaïs Nin spoke. Kathleen brought her home with a throng of others for M.F.K. Fischer's chicken soup and the Grey Riesling Charles picked out. We wanted Kathleen to go to Yale. She went instead to an apartment in San Rafael and worked in a land title company and would only cross the street at the corner and then not until the light turned green.

She loved Dan and fought with him until finally they tired and withdrew to separate corners.

On school breaks J.R. went On The Road as a gofer goaded into a dog-trot by Izzy Bleckman's annoyed shouts of 'Today!', J.R. being a cool dude and not used to hurrying. He wandered the back roads with Charles, saw the South through the eyes of a gandy-dancer, plied the waters of New England on a sailing sloop, headed West on the Oregon Trail. He was a child of his times, and in Marin drugs were as fashionable as dirty Reeboks. Timothy Leary's war cry, tune in, turn on, and drop out, were as much a part of his teen years as smoking a cigarette with Ed Muskie while waiting for the elevator at the Democratic convention. J.R.'s grades wouldn't let him into the universities I had in mind. Charles got him into Prescott, an alternative college in Arizona. When it closed, J.R. migrated to Evergreen State College up in Washington.

A volunteer firefighter at Evergreen's McLane Station 93 as an undergrad, J.R. and a buddy, Tommy Skjervold, nicked the siren off the station's fire engine. They concocted a scheme to send ransom notes to the chief, mailing them from obscure towns throughout the country. At one point J.R. explained to me the situation didn't look good, the chief's patience was running thin. To my delight, he insisted he was determined to take complete responsibility for the affair. Noble, I thought. I spoke to Tommy about J.R.'s decision.

Tommy was outraged at my take on the situation. 'J.R. better take the rap. It was his idea.'

Shannon was the one who claimed Marin for her own, running with a prancing pride of youngsters. There was the beautiful black-haired Troy; Kim of the perfect manners; the deceptively level-headed Mindy of the five Mahoneys. Shannon grew up as carefree as a Pacific zephyr. She fell in love with Dora Maar and, while hating Picasso, choose New York with its spectacular exhibit that summer for her high school graduation gift. She went on to Washington and the Hay-Adams whose rooms, she complained, were dreadfully small. She followed J.R. to Evergreen, but like Kathleen eventually graduated from Mills College in Oakland.

Charles saw Shannon on Broadway. She has the voice, he said, and is a natural actress, but she must want it. Her piano recitals of Paderewski and Beethoven, her drama courses with Shaw and Buchner, a lunch at New York's Four Seasons restaurant sitting across the placid black pool from John Gielgud were delicious little bonbons, but Shannon went her own way. In passing she handed us a piece of rice paper rich with watercolors of blues and browns and greens: 'In the quiet of the new fallen snow a woman walks along the shore of an emerald bay, eyes sparkling.'

Charles and I shared beliefs on what it means to lead a good life. We wanted the children to believe as we did. We had a tough time in part because our lives tended to be so scattered, in part because neither of us was any good at laying down the law. I lamented my lack of influence to Kathleen once. She was indignant at the assertion that none of the three ever listened to me, protesting with some fervor: 'We all pick up litter on the beach.' When I look at them, how different they are as if they had been raised in separate families, I suppose I should be thankful I can lay claim to an environmental bent if nothing else.

Our own parents molded Charles and me to a degree we never even came close to with my children. I suspect Charles' views carry little weight with his girls either, but this may be because they were adopted into their new family and had few opportunities to see what he was like up close. He spent summer holidays with them sailing the Caribbean or fishing on Western dude ranches. I have photos taken when they were quite young scampering across a North Carolina beach with their grandfather trudging behind. The girls sent Charles boxes of chocolates, Whitman's Samplers, for Christmas each year when they were tiny, graduating into more permanent gifts as they grew older. I have a small, folding brass easel from them sitting on a table at Derrynavglaun holding the photo of the day. Charles loved Susan and Lisa, but he had little impact on their daily routines.

Charles' early childhood was tranquil. Mine was turbulent. Charles joked about being a traveler before he was born chalking up fifty miles on the road as his father drove his mother an hour or so from the Onslow County farm to the hospital in Wilmington, North Carolina. I had a few miles under my belt as well. Mother's taxi driver took a wrong turn. I was almost born in Tijuana, Mexico instead of San Diego, California. Daddy didn't arrive for a couple of days. He was out prospecting for gold in Searchlight, Nevada.

Mother set up housekeeping in San Diego as Daddy sank shafts in the deserts of the Southwest dreaming of the big strike. Not long after I arrived, a letter from Daddy containing a bus ticket landed her in Las Vegas. At the height of the Great Depression, the construction of Boulder Dam was changing a wide spot in the road into a booming oasis.

When Mother arrived, Daddy was back out prospecting in Searchlight. She checked into a hotel on Fremont Street, confiding to the clerk that her husband would be arriving in a day or two.

A week passed. No one appeared. Another week went by. The bill was reaching alarming proportions. The hotel's owner sizing up the situation erroneously but benignly, invited Mother into his office for a chat. He had a proposition. He owned, he said, an auto court at the edge of town. A two-room adobe apartment did double duty as living quarters and office. There was plenty of room for the kids to play, mostly gravel, but a perverse patch of untamed grass skulked along the front walk. It was a quiet place. Construction workers and their friends would check in for an hour or two during the day just to get out of the blazing sun or for a quick snooze before heading back to the dam after a night on the town. The take for a night's rent on the twelve cabins was money in the bank. That was good enough for him. If a manager wanted to work a little harder, rent out a vacated room a second time, it was no concern of his. Was she interested?

By the time Daddy emerged from a cacti copse, Mother wore the mantle of prosperous entrepreneur. Accepting the hotel owner's offer with only a pinch of misgiving, she kept a respectable distance from the young men checking into the motel with their saucy serai. Roberta was in school. I skittered across the gravel courtyard on my hands and feet like a spider, trying to keep up as she changed bedding, scoured sinks, checked in customers and carefully pocketed newly-minted silver dollars. Roosevelt's abandonment of the gold standard, a source of constant despair for Daddy, was received with all the joy of a fresh rain by Mother eking out an existence in the parched Nevada desert.

Mother and Daddy joined the Vegas Bedouins dancing to the intoxicating rhythm of Charlie Pride and his band. Garlands of beads swayed on the lithe, lost girls dancing the Charleston with men whose cuffed trousers flicked across glossy wing-tips. In the cool of the morning, Daddy drove Charlie Pride down Fremont Street, Charlie bowing and waving to his fans. From Main to Fifth out into the desert, the echo of the hit of the day reverberated after them: 'Don't let foolish pride keep you from my side.'

Women loved Charlie Pride. And made money for him. Undisciplined, unself-conscious, Charlie's Pride burst forth, prickly desert blooms, lasting but a day.

Daddy and his best friend, Chuck Barbee, gathered together enough money to buy a parcel of land with a couple of gas pumps and a wooden shack. Mother was on to a new career. She pumped gas while Chuck and Daddy prospected. The stony arrowhead joining Fifth and Main at the junction of Route 66 would one day be the opening wedge to the Las Vegas Strip. Prescient as ever, Daddy saw the station only as a funnel for mining operations. He never recognized the value of real estate unless a vein of ore streaked through it.

Our tiny tribe sought relief from the broiling desert sun among giant Ponderosas on the slopes of Mt. Charleston. The mountain's craggy head surveying the arid wasteland from a breathtaking 11,918 feet, jabbed unsuspecting clouds like a banderillero and robbed them of their moisture. Mother's tiny Brownie caught the moment. She, daring in loose slacks and open, careless blouse. Daddy challenging.

Lean, handsome Chuck. Serious Roberta, hands clasped. Chubby me. The ever present cloth-covered roadster. We were so smart and so young and so happy.

And, somewhere far away on a Southern farm, Wallace and Ina Kuralt were young and happy, and Charles was aborning.

Caught up in the Depression as we were, Charles's parents, college graduates in an already poor Southern state, made the best of it. For a time they lived with Mrs. Kuralt's parents, John and Rena Bishop, on their small tobacco farm in Onslow county, North Carolina. After the young family moved into a home of their own, Charles continued to spend summers with his grandparents. The talk, the neighborliness, the easy, slow rhythms of the rural South were a comfort to a small boy beset with quickness and itchy feet. His grandfather, John Bishop, might annoy his wife by sitting under a leafy tree in his old overalls telling stories, but for Charles the moments were pure pleasure. Rena Bishop, a proud woman with an ingrained sense of the rightness of things, brought structure to Charles' early education reading the American classics to him on the front porch swing. He saw his grandmother cry when the rural electrification scheme, the REA, brought electricity to the farm. The sight turned him into a lifelong liberal.

Money was hard to come by on the farm, but there was no lack of contentment rising out of a surety of one's place, a stability in one's surroundings, the familiarity of it all. In Conamara today people look at the dizzying change of pace and ask, 'What good is money if you lose your comfort?' In the Thirties, it was a sentiment Charles along with many rural Southerners echoed. Charles believed too much weight is given money as a measure of success. Some people inherit wealth; others inherit poverty. Lazy people are wealthy. People who work hard are broke. Charles was not, however, blind to the hopelessness of crushing poverty. In 1987 he wrote the lyrics for *Tobacco Warehouse Blues*, 'Sal, you ain't' gonna get no rockin' chair … ,' a poignant evocation of the relentless struggle for survival in much of the rural South. Charles witnessed the despair first hand.

Material success was not important to Charles' father either. Mr. Kuralt left Massachusetts to attend the University of North Carolina. He met Ina Bishop there and decided to stay. He went to work for the government convinced that good men could use institutions to change things for the better. A career devoted to social work brought him great satisfactions but didn't make him wealthy. After his death Charles helped raise money to endow the Wallace Kuralt Chair at the University of North Carolina's School of Social Work. Reserved and unassuming, this is, perhaps, the one honor of which Mr. Kuralt would have approved.

Ina Bishop left her family's tobacco farm to go to college taking a degree in home economics. She taught school after Charles was born to help make ends meet leaving Charles in the care of a kindly black woman whom he came to love. Charles spoke of one cheerful afternoon spent busily cutting up a brightly-colored quilt, when he should have been napping, as a surprise for his Mother. His thrill of creativity was greeted with mild consternation by both women. It is telling that Charles recalled the occasion with enjoyment and not a modicum of contrition.

Strong bonds between young white children nursed by attentive black women were not unusual in the South when Charles was growing up. This frequent arrangement of childcare may have spun off an unanticipated bonus in the form of support for the Civil Rights movement. At UNC Charles, editor of the *Daily Tar Heel*, used the student newspaper to make early and repeated calls for the end of segregation.

In his views on race, Charles emulated his father. Wallace Kuralt looked at a flawed world, chose an injustice, and sat about correcting it. His pragmatic solutions to welfare problems were sold to doubting Southerners with a panache revealing a cheerful strain of showmanship. The North Carolina legislature about to vote a decrease in payments to welfare mothers and their children, most of whom were black, received a visit on the floor of the lower chamber from Papa Kuralt. He had in tow several small children and a band of reporters. The next day newspapers all over the state carried pictures of smiling representatives dandling cherubic youngsters on their knees. The welfare cut was defeated. Comparing his career to his father's, Charles would dispiritedly point out that his father made the world better and never made any money, while, he, Charles, was paid a great deal for doing almost nothing

Mr. Kuralt's view of parenting dictated preparing a child to leave the nest. Like Daedalus, he taught his son to fly. My own father wanted nothing so much as to keep me constantly in view. For both of us, our fathers' affection was constant and complete. It is bewildering to me now that Charles and I would so casually deprive our own children of that immense, sheltering influence. Judith Wallerstein, a woman I met in Belvedere, began the first long-term study on the consequences of divorce on children. She quoted to damning effect a small boy she had interviewed. 'I know divorce is good for my mommy, and it's good for my daddy, but it's not good for me.'

A Birthday Poem for Shannon

Now she is 18, and we're not ready...
The experience, as always, is slightly heady,
Now, she is 18, and looking fine...
But 18 is double 9.

She was only 9 when I first ~~amtxhmpx~~ knew her,
~~Exekzbeforexakexfxlledzmmxzkerzmmakerzx~~
Now she's twice as old and bolder and ~~txexxbimmrzxpxmerzx~~ bluer
~~amdxtxiierzmmdzxixerzxz~~ And twice as wise and taller and truer
But 18 is double 9.

Time, in its flight, does not seem to tarry...
Now she can vote and now she can marry...
Though I hope she'll listen to me and her mother,
And do the one, and not the other...

~~Amdxgmztexsxhmetzx~~

For, though she is 18, we're not ready...
We know she's bright and pretty and steady...
Today she is 18, and that's just fine...
But 18 is double 9.

We remember the birthdays that hurried past us
~~Thexommmriexzthatxwillxzkexextmzimxtxmszxz~~
Our memories are enough to last us...
Every easter egg and Christmas wreath...
And the ~~brmxexzxhmzmorexomzkerzkexthzxzx~~ silver braces she wore on her teeth.

And the songs and the games and the boy chasing,
And the late, late nights and the midnight pacing,
When she said she'd be home by half past 10...
And was out past 3 again.

Well, now she is 18, and that's behind us...
She doesn't have to listen or mind us...
But no matter how you cut it, or fry it it, or boil it...
She's got her own house -- but it's still our toilet...
                    (SPOKEN:)
Now -- you are 18... Have your kicks,
But remember twice 9 is half 36 ---
Now you are 18, and that's just swell...
It's the age to start treating old folks well ...

                    (SINGING:)

Cause... Now ~~youxarex18zx~~ you are 18...~~frmazxzrexpiendmmkz~~ and full of
                                        resplendence,
In your freedom, your independence,
Now you are 18, we know that's nice..
But to us, you're just 9 twice...

And though you reside on the hill above us,
We hope you'll continue to call... And love us --
~~Youxrexofficialiyzmzmomanzimxthexmmrldyzmhiriziyzxz~~
~~Emtxtmzmsyzx~~
Cause no matter how many calendar pages
Turn, and no matter what your age is...
   No matter that Kathleen and Dan and J.R. -- Are grown, we know how old they
No matter that you're a woman in the worldly whirl --   are
You're still our little girl!

HAPPY BIRTHDAY TO YOU......

On the West Coast a seismic tremor shattered our family's predilection for rosy outlooks no matter what. The quake struck without warning, strewing our complacences over a darkened landscape. In the upheaval, the agreeable distinction between good guys and bad guys collapsed. The faultline was not a bold break but a jagged tear. There is no sympathy in this world for outlaws. Perhaps, that is as it should be. But if you don't walk away, you may find yourself trapped like Alice behind the looking glass. Life becomes a series of grotesqueries. Certainty gives way to confusion. For five years we struggled to make sense of what happened, to make it all right again. In the end, we failed. When I am asked why we did it, why we stayed the course, I quote Matthew, chapter 25, verse 36. It is Jesus speaking to his disciples, ' … I was in prison and ye came to me.'

He was tall. 6'2". Angular. Weighed in at 175 pounds. A nice WASP face. Chiseled nose, wide, thin lips. When I first met him he was a laid-back Californian picking up tabs at chic little restaurants where the staff greeted him as a prodigal son. Douglas was polite and charming with a certain worldliness but little formal education. He felt no need of it. Life was quite all right. He fell in love with one of my daughters. When I mentioned a particular preference for an old friend whose cooking skills knocked me out, Douglas looked me in the eye and said, 'I can learn to cook.'

A gang of us were back at Tahoe for Christmas. Charles was arriving later than usual. I staggered through a little something from Julia Child for a midnight supper which took three days to prepare not counting the shopping and frequent referrals to both volumes I and II of *Mastering the Art of French Cooking*. Craig Claiborne, the *New York Times* food critic, later wrote that *Garniture de Volaille, Financière* (diced chicken in white-wine sauce with quenelles, truffles, mushrooms and olives served in a large vol-au-vent) was impossible to produce in a home kitchen. Not impossible, maybe, but requiring, certainly, a span of single-mindedness maddening to anyone who assumes an 'It's only a dinner, for heaven's sake' attitude. Douglas who was to join us was away on business in Mexico City but sent bottles of two great French wines, a Margaux and a Haut-Brion. Charles arrived, after grim hours waiting for late planes, with a splitting migraine. Everyone else's appetite had been deadened by twelve hours of snacking. It was a moment an amateur cook never forgets.

In a week or two I learned Douglas was not in Mexico City but in Lima, Peru. He had been arrested in the port city of Callao with a packet containing one kilogram of cocaine strapped to each ankle. Pedro de Cieza de León, a Spanish conquistador marching through Peru with Francisco Pizzaro in 1532, wrote in his memoir, *The Incas:* 'This coca was so valuable in Peru in the years 1548, 1549, and 1551 that there never was in the whole world a plant … so highly valued.' For the Western world the enigmatic coca plant posed a dilemma at first tantalizing whiff.

It was a Saturday afternoon when I called Charles. He was in New York writing the Sunday show. Charles knew Peru. As CBS Latin American correspondent he became inured to the parade of grasping dictators, bands of ragged revolutionaries, the senseless poverty that bedeviled the continent. It was he who first quoted to me Simon Bolivar's melancholy remark made when close to death, 'We have plowed the sea.' Now considered the greatest South American revolutionary, the Liberator defeated Spain, freeing the land from its colonial past, only to die poor and bitterly hated.

Charles was interested in almost everything, but he was not interested in the drug war. He did a story, an hour documentary, I think, early in his career at CBS. He was persuaded to try the drug of the day, marijuana or, maybe, cocaine. Whatever it was, he didn't like it, and he didn't try it again, not that drug or any other. When he wanted to climb down from the adrenaline high he lived on most of his life, he drank scotch or gin or vodka. He was a chain smoker. Wherever he was, a carton of Pall Malls was close at hand.

While Charles never advocated abolition of the drug laws, it was obvious to him they do little good. Protecting Americans while demolishing the lives of Peruvian or Colombian or Bolivian peasants is a zero sum game. Charles had a strong libertarian streak. He objected to government telling him how to conduct his personal life. He didn't want anyone else telling him how to live, either. He was infuriated by proselytizers of various health fads. He thought jogging inane. Ate what he wanted. Refused to visit homes where he was requested to remove his shoes or refrain from smoking.

Deemed it bad manners if your host handed you a glass of wine instead of a martini before sitting down to dinner.

When I told him Douglas was in a Peruvian jail, Charles didn't give me a lecture about the rights and wrongs of the situation. He called Jody Marek, the press officer at the American Embassy in Lima, to tell him we were on our way. Then, he went out and picked up airline schedules from Braniff and Varig. He warned me about the *guara*, the soft, cold Lima drizzle. He explained the Peruvian money system, the *sol*, and how we would be looked upon as rich Yankees. He became excited recounting the discovery of the famed Inca fortress, Manchu Pichu, by Hiram Bingham in 1911. In typical Charles fashion, he urged us to stay at the premier Gran Hotel Bolivar on the Plaza San Martin. Charles knew, but he didn't tell me, we weren't going to get Douglas out of Peru.

I called Ed Allison with whom I worked in Carson City when he served as Paul Laxalt's press secretary. Ed went to D.C. when the Governor won the Senate race after a brief sojourn as a private citizen. I suspect Ed, too, knew we were on a quixotic journey, but he and Paul did all they could. The Senator sent a telegram to Frank Ortiz, our Ambassador: 'Would greatly appreciate any assistance you can give ... when she contacts the Embassy.' Ed's call to Jody Marek followed Charles'.

By the time Kathleen and Shannon arrived in Lima, I had written to every newsman and human rights advocate I ever met. Herb Caen at the *San Francisco Chronicle* sent a quick pundit's take, 'Gad, the frustration.' Frank McCulloch, Executive Editor at McClatchy Newspapers, sighed, 'I wish very much that I could think of something to suggest ...' Amnesty International's Ruth Weil replied, 'We have received numerous complaints about … (Peruvian) prisons … ' Even Peru's Justice Minister Enrique Elias Laroza was complaining, 'Peruvian prisons aren't bad, they're horrible.'

I did discover a few facts from a mix of Consul-Generals, Ambassadors and private attorneys with a hint or two thrown in from a few San Franciscans who probably had it right. The legals laid out the routine. You are arrested by the Guardia Civil. You are kept *incommunicado* during a fifteen day interrogation period. While you are in prison, a minimum five month investigation may be extended on a month to month basis. An attorney is brought in at the end of the investigation for a series of tribunal appearances over an indeterminate amount of time. There was no defense for drug offenses, so the best an attorney could do was work for a lighter sentence or a smaller fine. His primary function was to insure the case didn't get bogged down indefinitely. After sentencing, drug cases are automatically reviewed by the Supreme Court. If everything is in order, the international prisoner is eligible for exchange under signed treaties. If you're lucky, you're looking at twenty-four months.

A little color was added by the extra-legals. Fifteen days in interrogation means fifteen days of torture. Beatings by both guards and other prisoners are a way of life. On truly bad days buses pull up outside the Lima prison, El Sexto. Armed men pour out, hurling themselves through the big double gates, usually closed, now thrown wide open. The beatings of the men and the plundering of their meager possessions is a part of prison discipline. The *Internationales* laugh and swear at the stupidity of the marauding soldiers and at their own bravado. When they are herded into the open patio, the tattered men bring with them a precious belonging or two, letters, a pair of shoes, a cheap AM wireless. They defy the soldiers, turning the requisa into a game of wits, throwing the bundles through the barred gates, sprinting through the gauntlet. It happens every few weeks.

If you are a Peruvian, most likely a Quechua Indian, in prison, your family keeps you alive. The women stand in line for several hours three or four times a week carrying baskets of food, a clean shirt, a few *soles* to pay for a bed. On visiting days, the newest baby is added to the pile. If you are an *Internationale,* you better have money and a friend in the Embassy to bring it to you, plus attorneys, stateside and Peruvian. Count on a hundred thousand dollars. Don't bother to ask about time. It could take years.

Hardly a day went past without a news story in the American press about cocaine. More than fifteen million Americans had used the drug. Admissions to drug clinics had tripled in the past five years. Every drug bust set a new record. In March of '82 a billion dollars worth of cocaine, over 1,700 kilos, was seized in Miami. It was on an airport cargo dock marked 'blue jeans.' The war on drugs was debated endlessly. Even the *Scientific American* took a stand:

> Along with nicotine and caffeine, cocaine is a plant alkaloid carrying considerable pharmacological effect first known to the Indians of the New World. Had the coca leaf found its way into the world market as the tobacco leaf and coffee bean did, cocaine might occupy a very different place in today's custom and culture.

Charles was following Peru closely now and noticed an increase in activity of the Sendero Luminoso, the Luminous Path, a shadowy guerrilla group operating high in the Andes. They were becoming bolder, coming closer and closer to Lima. They claimed to be Chinese Marxists, which led some lowlanders in Lima to the conclusion that the mountains were rife with Chinese revolutionaries. Sendero Luminoso was a homegrown group led by a philosophy professor at the University of Ayacucho, Abimail Guzmán. Whatever it was he wanted, he didn't get. He is at present in a remote Peruvian prison, whereabouts uncertain.

Down in Lima Kathleen and Shannon ignored Charles' pleas to stay at the Gran Hotel Bolivar. They moved into Atahualpa House in Miraflores, directed there by Jody Marek. The girls took a room on the first floor of the crumbling colonial-style home turned pensión by its owner, Señora Pilar. The water came and went as it pleased, the room remained uncleaned, but it was a good choice for a couple of reasons. The disparity between the Bolivar and the prison would have been unbearable. Secondly, there was a safety at Atahualpa House. In a strange way we became a part of the family. Señora Pilar and her haughty mother and her sophisticated daughter, Ari, were remnants of a minuscule middle-class, educated, worldly, absolutely broke. One evening which no one in this family will forget, an officer in the Guardia Civil banged on the door demanding the family surrender a family heirloom, an ancient alpaca rug. A national treasure, the officer maintained, which must be returned to the people of Peru. Loot, contended Ari, shouting abuse at the guard and his pack of thieves, eventually driving him from the door through the gardens and into the street, where, Ari coolly murmured, he belonged.

I was still at Tahoe when Sendero Luminoso struck Lima blowing up power stations, turning much of the city into an inky labyrinth. After frantic attempts to reach Atahualpa House, I finally got through to Shannon. She was nonchalant. It was no worse than the earthquake which rattled the city a few days earlier knocking stucco cornices off buildings in the old section of Lima where she had been visiting a rug maker, one of the famous Sulka family. I had been urging the girls to make use of their time in Peru to learn the culture, reading off museum locations and library hours from the travel books Charles sent. Until I stayed in Lima myself, I was never quite satisfied with their protestations that nothing was open when I said it was going to be or maybe not open at all, so my reaction to this latest bit of news was mixed at best. I asked to speak to Kathleen. She wasn't there. She was down at the clinic getting her leg looked at. What, I asked, was the matter with Kathleen's leg. Well, they had been out shopping when the power station was blown up. In the darkness Kathleen fell into a pothole taking a chunk of flesh out of her shin. I had a flashback to the not-so-long-ago nights when Charles and I climbed groggily into the car, driving over the Golden Gate bridge to pick up one of the kids after a concert at Bill Graham's Filmore West, convinced it was too dangerous for them to drive themselves home.

For the next couple of years, we became like the Quechua women, waiting, singly or in pairs, outside the prison to take food or medicine or money into Douglas. The girls cooked pots of soup, cheap vegetable broths with fancy names like minestrone and vichyssoises in Señora Pilar's cramped kitchen. They argued with sharp-eyed sellers at the *mercado* battling over half a *centavo* on the price of a mango or guava. In one of their long, frantic walks they discovered a health food shop run by two sweet-faced Peruvian girls and stocked up on vitamins and beeswax candles, these last for Douglas' improbable meditations.

Standing in the midst of chattering Quechua women, hot, dusty, anxious that the small door should open and that there be no buses filled with Guardia Civil today, please not today, you learn the meaning of the word impassive. When the hour of admittance has come and gone, and the long line of women has grown angry, the captain of the guards begins his slow saunter up the line, stamping a number, or maybe two or three, in black on each brown forearm. The phalanx of guards tire of brandishing their sub-machine guns. An eternity later that small door opens. Inside a second contingent of guards demand passports causing, always, my heart to sink. We go down a dark, moldy hallway where two old women sit patting the young wives and heavy-set mothers filing past. They search for knives or the few *soles* the women have scraped together to bring to their men.

Slipping through a maze of walkways and doorways, we climb a steep spiral staircase to the solitary cubicle housing the foreigners. The tubercular dampness that fills the city's hospitals to over-flowing, clutches at the prisoners. The high, small window, a builder's sly joke, offers no relief, catching neither sunlight nor breeze. Double bunks line the walls. Built for the small, wiry Quechuas, the beds are too short by a foot for the Europeans. The gaunt, fatigued men crouch on the hard pallets or shuffle crab-like down the narrow aisle between the rows of beds.

We got to know them all. They were from New Zealand, Holland, England, the States. Most were in their thirties. One gray-haired man from Southern California was the subject of long, sobbing telephone calls from his distraught mother. A sister of a handsome Don Juan was alternately terrified for his safety and rabid that his attorneys were taking every cent she made. A joyless poet from outside London had neither friends nor family nor attorney. If he managed to stay alive, he would be there a very long time. I sent a card to Steve which I found in a high-priced Marin card shop. A cartoon drawing of the Welsh explorer H.M. Stanley finding the Scottish missionary David Livingstone near death on the shores of Lake Tanganyika carried the caption: 'Still living, I presume.' At the time I found it absolutely hilarious.

More sobering was the plaque I stopped to read while aimlessly wandering across the dunes at Point Reyes National Seashore, a few miles north of San Francisco. The wild crocus bloomed and the gull cried. I was on Drake's beach where, perhaps, Sir Francis Drake put ashore on the Incredible Voyage begun in 1577 and ending in 1580. Drake's trip girdling the earth began in Plymouth, England, took him around the tip of South America and up the Pacific coast pillaging and plundering as he went. The plaque read:

In the principal port of Peru, Callao de Lima, seven ships are set adrift, others raided. Here Drake undertakes a risky land excursion in an attempt to free a long time friend from a prison of the Inquisition. Unhappily, he must retreat.

The French composer, Jacque Offenbach, three centuries later in 1868 based his opera, *La Perichole*, on Drake's rescue attempt.

We didn't bring Douglas home. We have the Sendero Luminoso to thank for that. The *San Francisco Examiner* reported in May of 1983: 'Leftist rebels bombed 10 Lima electric towers and set off scores of bombs near the US Embassy and other capital targets in a night-time onslaught … Parts of the capital were blacked out for 90 minutes … there were casualties.'

One of those casualties was Douglas. He was out of his cell walking one of the dank, damp corridors when the lights went off. A tall man among the small statured Quechuas, he was a menacing shadow to the frightened guard who shot him. The bullet went through his ear shattering his cheek-bone. The Peruvians sent him home where he was re-tried and re-sentenced.

Charles and I flew up to spend the week-end with Douglas on his first two-day pass from prison. He lurched a little, his laugh was strained, but he was home. He was full of reminiscence, not of Peru, but of earlier days, stories of outwitting the law with small cargoes of marijuana. They were Prohibition tales straight out of the Thirties, bold as a kick of Appalachia moonshine. Outmaneuvering Drug Enforcement Administration planes to land on boggy patches of the Everglades. Striking up a conversation with the same Canadian Mountie each time he crossed the border just to see if he could get away with it. Giving away whatever money there was. Charles chuckled as I laughed uproariously. We thought the worst was over. For us it had just begun. Douglas ran. He came back to us for a few days. Then, early one afternoon he strolled into an open field. There among the grasses he sat down, assumed his yoga pose and shot himself.

We sailed out under the Golden Gate bridge scattering his ashes on the sea. Charles read the eulogy, a poem he knew in his youth.

> With whinnying, snorting, contorting and prancing,
> As you dodged your pursuers, looking askance,
> With Greek-footed figures, and Parthenon paces,
> O broncho that would not be broken of dancing.

I don't begrudge Douglas his death, but suicide marks those left behind. There are always questions. There are never answers.

San Fran-cis-co Stocks. An idea waiting to be discarded.

We launched into it with our customary damn-the-torpedoes approach. No experience, no marketing surveys, no cost analysis. Lots of enthusiasm. The blueprint was a new book, Raymond Sokolov's *The Saucier's Apprentice.* A triumph of marketing, Mr. Sokolov's soaring prose stretched twelve pages from *The Joy of Cooking* into 213 sheets of fantasy. The idea that the best French cooking was the original fast food was a revelation. Mr. Sokolov explained with cooking stocks on hand scores of fabulous French sauces could be whipped up in minutes. We loved French sauces. Everyone loved French sauces. We would hand-make fat-free stocks, freeze them, sell them to a calorie conscious world. Gourmet cooking in minutes. It was better than the Instant Park. Upscale consumers, palates made sophisticated by years of watching Julia Child, would sweep them off the shelves. We would be rich.

We set to work. Without Kathleen, we set to work. Kathleen takes after her grandmother in this one respect. The woman who kept my family afloat had little interest in chasing rainbows. Kathleen, too, likes to feel the earth under her feet. J.R., on the other hand, could be roped into almost anything. He filled a yellow legal pad with calculations to determine the size of a delivery truck, the exact distance between carrying trays, the power output needed to prevent meltdown. I envisioned delivery in a wicker basket covered with a checkered cloth rather like our picnic basket. J.R. insisted that was not businesslike. He discussed our needs with half a dozen purpose-built truck manufacturers, piling up brochures on insulation and refrigerator units. Potential costs escalated. My basket retailed for $6.99 at Cost Plus. J.R.'s truck ran in the neighborhood of $30,000. The debate came to a halt when Charles persuaded us Izzy Bleckman had the right idea. Buy picnic lockers, throw in some dry ice and away you go. That's what we did for five years with never a thaw. We did invest in a new Volvo wagon to put the picnic lockers in. Image, I thought, was important, even if we didn't deliver in wicker baskets.

Charles called Chris Kerageorgiou, a New Orleans chef, and asked him to take on a saucier's apprentice. Stopping by New Orleans every chance he got, Charles knew all the best restaurants, but it was to La Provence across Lake Pontchartrain that he sent Shannon. Charles wrote in his *America* Mr. Kerageorgiou's sauces 'would make cardboard taste delicious.' We agreed we might as well start at the top.

Unlike Charles I didn't get to New Orleans often and always approached the city as a pilgrim to the font. While Charles was working I visited museums and wandered down to the river. We stayed in the old French Quarter. In the evenings we walked the tranquil streets made extravagant with ornate ironwork climbing the faded brick facades and drank in the fragrances escaping from high walled gardens. We ate our way through the city beginning at LeRuth's and

La Provence, but one evening after a day of speeches and cocktail parties, Charles suggested we go no further than the elevator and chance the hotel dining room. The menu offered multi-layered entrees of doubtful provenance, but the appetizers made our mouths water. Fresh oysters, puff paste *petite bouchees* oozing bits of shellfish and *millle-feuilles* bubbling with cheese, caviar. 'We will forego the entree,' Charles smiled at the waiter, 'and order, instead, several appetizers.' 'No,' replied our waiter. 'You can't do that. You must order an entree.'

I waited, wondering what my tired chevalier would say to that. They skirmished for a minute or two, Charles patiently explaining it was not the cost, that didn't matter, but we didn't want an entree, we wanted a variety of appetizers; the waiter was adamant and kept shaking his head, no. Quiet fell. I saw the look settle onto Charles' face. It was the 'just watch me' firming of the muscles that began somewhere deep down in his pysche when Charles bumped into a 'you can't do that.' He turned slightly in his chair, one hand dropped to his upper thigh, fingers spread, tips pushing slightly into the material of his trousers. The elbow of his other arm rested on the table, the fingers of that hand lightly stroking his chin. For a fraction of a second, his jaw clinched. He looked the waiter in the eye. 'I tell you what. You go back into the kitchen and pick out any two entrees you want. Put them on my bill.' Pause. 'Then, we will have ... ' The appetizers weren't bad, but the bill was astronomical.

Shannon had never been in New Orleans. Charles gave her a pep talk before putting her on a plane to Chris Kerageorgiou to see how stock-making worked in practice.

She found it an uncomplicated process. After a few days she arrived back in Marin with all the basics including an easy way to cool stock before packaging. Set it out on the back step. Be sure there aren't any animals around. She learned that not in the kitchen at La Provence but from wending her way through the city's back streets. Her education completed, her next assignment was to design a commercial kitchen, explore the used equipment shops, figure out how much money this enterprise was going to cost. She was the only one who had a clue as to what we needed.

I lined up an attorney and an accountant. J.R., relieved of the burden of setting up a delivery system, began the quest for a suitable location. We had taken a house at Inverness near the Point Reyes National Seashore after a year at Tahoe. I wanted the kitchen to be there, among the impromptu pergolas and greenhouses of the Birkenstocks and granny dress set. It was our milieu, lovingly-tended gardens, organic produce, bucolic landscape. An idyll of freshly cut parsley, opalescent mushrooms peeking out of a rich loam, fish carcasses retrieved from trawlers plying the sea. A local mover and shaker owned an empty dairy he was willing to lease us until the health department apprised him of certain changes he would have to make. I tried to persuade him to ignore all that red tape. He wouldn't. I was sorry about that. I hated to loose him. He would have been a fine landlord. A great talker, he told me, 'You keep comin' at me. I keep dancing away.' We ended up in a San Rafael industrial park cubicle, practical for delivery, but numbingly dull.

Still, we were moving right along.

From time to time Charles inquired wistfully, 'When are you going to make a batch of stock?'

I brushed the query aside. That was the least of our worries.

Marketing was what we belatedly began worrying about. We had the incredible good luck to stumble across a small design firm who understood the meaning of creativity on a shoe string. Leta did our six-ounce containers in gray and one color, each straight out of a turn of century Italian print: briny blue Fish Stock; sunset orange heralding the White; rich, earthy Brown Stock; pulsing pink for our jewel, our Demi-Glacé. We were going to call ourselves 'The Pacific Stock Exchange'. Our attorney said there might be legal problems. So, after little debate we settled on 'San Francisco Stocks.'

We were as surprised as anyone when San Francisco Stocks 'Stock Market' displays began springing up around the Bay Area. Smart lapels sported *I'm Bullish on San Francisco Stocks*' buttons. The best kitchens had copies of our 'Stock Options', updated recipes straight out of Shannon's test kitchen. Businesslike in Brooks Brothers button downs and starched white chef's aprons, we manned booths at food shows sheltered under bouquets of blue delphiniums and white spider mums growing over shiny copper pots. We ladled out Shrimp and Scallion Ravioli with Dill Sauce or Wild Rice and Red Snapper Soup to starving gourmands who showed up with glasses of chilled California chardonnay from the neighboring booth.

The San Francisco Stock's test kitchen was one of our best ideas. J.R. and I were the test panel. Shannon would whip up a feast, maybe, Julia Child's *Filet de Boeuf Braise*

Prince Albert (braised filet of beef stuffed with foie gras and truffles). We'd hold a referendum, declare a holiday, cover a table with our checked table cloth and assess the result. These bagatelles became days of celebration. On Thomas Jefferson's birthday, we read the Declaration of Independence. On St. Patrick's Day, we hummed along to Charles' *The Irish Uprising*. If nothing was going on that grabbed our attention, we sat around and told each other how great we were.

For all that, San Francisco Stocks was back-breaking. I was at the kitchen before six in the morning, cranking up Dietrich Fischer-Dieskau's *Don Giovanni* and filling the stock pots. It takes a hundred pounds of veal bones, browned slowly, turned often, for one batch of gelatinous brown. A hundred pounds of fish carcasses have to be gutted for the fish stock. The white stock was relatively easy. You threw in vegetables with backs and wings. Everything was done by hand, chopping, straining, sautéing, skimming. The demi-glacé was simmered and reduced for three days with bottles of Madeira poured in at the last. And, oh, the cleaning, the scrubbing and the mopping. It was the hardest work I have ever done.

Standing over the steam kettles, skimming the froth from the stock, Mother would lose patience with me. She would begin interrogating me. 'Pat, why are you doing this?' To drive home her point, she would throw in the clincher. 'You are paying to do this?' This last was a reference to the red ink on our bottom line.

San Francisco Stocks brought me one treasure. It was the friendship of an extraordinary woman, M.F.K. Fisher, Mary Francis to her friends. She was a writer and a cook, a polished sophisticate, totally charming, unpretentious, absolutely authentic. M.F.K. Fisher attained cult status among the cognoscenti, but never made a best seller list. It was Mary Francis' chicken soup we served to Anaïs Nin when Ms. Nin accompanied Kathleen home after she spoke to Women On The Move. Mary Francis lived in Glen Ellen in an adobe house, tile-roofed, on a patch of ground set aside for her by the adoring owner of a large estate. A big cheerful room housed her books, her plain oak dining table, her range, her overstuffed chairs. She received callers who came to pay her homage with warmth and humor, cooking them dinner, shoving aside the dirty dishes, eager for conversation. Mary Francis' goodbyes were always said at her gate, she leaning gracefully against it, her hands clasped together, a sweet smile on her face, a portrait for her guest to take home.

I don't remember what she prepared for lunch that first spring day when I arrived clutching a basket with a black truffle nestling inside. I do remember gushing over her culinary skills. Her reaction was rueful. I'm a lot better writer than I am a cook, she said. It was an unaffected recognition of the arbitrariness of fame and fortune. When success arrived, it had been miserly enough, and it didn't put in an appearance until the party was almost over. Mary Francis wasn't bitter about the delay, but she was a bit baffled by how it all worked. I was no use to her. I could only shake my head in consternation.

A Californian by birth, Mary Francis spent much of her life in France, sometimes married, at other times with her two daughters, occasionally alone. She spent a few days in Reno in the early sixties arriving on the train, her hair up in that elegant chignon, make-up in place, make-up case in hand. I believe Reno proved too brassy for her taste. The feminist movement was a trifle too brassy for her as well. Sure of herself and her abilities, she couldn't conceive of someone restraining her against her will. She found the Peru conundrum more intellectually stimulating than the agitated struggles of house-bound females. When Peru swamped me, Mary Francis was my life preserver.

I wanted Charles to do a piece on her. She wasn't his kind of story—she was far too urbane—but *Sunday Morning* was strong on the arts. I begged him to come to lunch at Glen Ellen. Discomfited by the thought of possible intrusion, Charles at last yielded on the condition I not mention a possible story. Mary Francis was happy to meet him, but didn't know who he was. She didn't watch television. I had been hesitant to explain who he was. She and Charles chatted about this and that, uncertain where they were supposed to be going, Mary Francis trying to draw Charles out, and Charles, the quintessential interviewer, unable to find out much about her. They agreed that Jack London, who had lived in Glen Ellen, was a fine regional writer but not much more. There was impassioned disagreement over the merits of Eudora Welty. Charles admired her as a writer and as a woman of the South. Mary Francis insisted Ms. Welty's time was past, maintaining her last book was an old woman's book, a remark startling to me and maddening to Charles.

We parted after a pleasant though somewhat unsatisfactory afternoon, me frustrated, Charles bemused, leaving behind a puzzled Mary Francis with a pile of dirty dishes.

After all this time it is still hard for me to believe the world was not ready for San Francisco Stocks. We never made any money. We had a dozen or so upscale markets around the Bay area, Balducci's in New York. Balducci's was a prime seller for us. J.R. maintained Charles went in every Saturday and cleaned out the shelves. Charles denied the accusation, and I never believed it. The hard truth was we were too expensive for a mass market. We couldn't get the price down and keep the quality up. Reading the handwriting on the wall, first, Shannon, and then J.R., peeled off. I thought about getting an employee or two, but I couldn't afford decent salaries. A friend suggested hiring undocumented workers, but I rebelled at the thought. Didn't I learn '*Which side are you on, boys?*' at my Daddy's knee?

I kept it up for one more year before deciding Mother was right. It wasn't smart. I was using muscles I never knew I had, working fifteen-hour days. Losing money as fast as I could. It was time to quit. I haven't had a decent Sauce Madere since.

STOCK OPTIONS No. 12

WILD RICE AND RED SNAPPER SOUP

People who insist they hate fish love this aromatic, easy to prepare soup.
Serves 2

2 containers SFS Fish Stock
1/4 cup wild rice
1/4 lb red snapper
1 clove garlic
1 shallot
1-1/2 Tbs butter

Finely chop the shallot and garlic. Sauté in butter. Add to simmering Fish Stock. Add wild rice. Boil gently 45 minutes to 1 hour until rice is done. Add red snapper, cut into 1/2 inch dice. Cook 3 to 5 minutes until fish flakes with a fork.

NO. 24

STOCK OPTIONS

SHRIMP AND SCALLION RAVIOLI WITH DILL SAUCE

We read about a group of New York chefs who use won ton skins to make ravioli and decided to try it ourselves. This is the result. At informal get-togethers we keep a pot of Fish Stock simmering and let the guests cook their own. It is a marvelous way to put a little movement into a party especially if the group is not well-acquainted. Serves 4 to 6.

RAVIOLI

9 oz shrimp meat
3 scallions
1 Tbs lemon juice
48 won ton skins
4 containers SFS Fish Stock

Chop shrimp meat coarsely and scallions finely. Mix with lemon juice. Place a rounded teaspoon of filling on won ton skin. Moisten edge with a mixture of beaten egg yolk and 1 teaspoon water. Cover with second skin. Press together with the blunt edge of a pastry ring to seal. Further seal by pressing together with fingertips. Cut out ravioli with pastry ring. Cook about 1 minute in 4 thawed containers of Fish Stock which have been brought to a low boil.

Please Turn Over

DILL SAUCE

2 Tbs butter
2 Tbs flour
1 container SFS Fish Stock which has been brought to a boil
1/2 cup cream
1 Tbs fresh dill, finely chopped
1 tsp lemon juice
Salt to taste

Make a velouté by melting butter 'til foam subsides, whisking in flour and stirring over medium heat for a couple of minutes, then slowly whisk in hot Fish Stock. Let cook over low heat stirring constantly about 5 minutes or until thick. Add cream, dill, lemon juice and salt. Return to simmer. Spoon over ravioli.

With the giddiness of San Francisco Stocks folding like a frothy egg white into the feverish Peruvian morass, life was verging on the maniacal. We made tentative efforts to settle down.

'Calm,' Charles would say, 'if not happy.'

Ireland beckoned. We bought Derrynavglaun.

Charles had never been to the Emerald Isle. I felt shy, showing him around. It was he, always, who introduced me to new things. I chose Irish country houses for us to stay in, clusters of welcoming rooms with sweetly-scented urns of potpourri tucked into hallway niches and offerings of wild Irish salmon and blackberry fool for dinner. We traveled south from Dublin, circling to the West. When we reached Conamara, we checked into Cashel House, sank into a deep sofa before a turf fire and vowed never to leave.

The forty miles from Galway town to Cashel was not the ramble I promised Charles it would be. The lure of Conamara for me was its emptiness, its untamed beauty. When I first drove the narrow, unlaned roads, there were times I didn't see another car for miles at a stretch. I drove the coast route, stopping at a farmhouse to pick up the key to Padraig Pearse's small cottage located a bit over, toward the sea. Walking up the rough path to the whitewashed stone dwelling, windswept and barren, I thought, yes, this is the poet's place. Grand dreams were aswirl in the air. His time here turned Padraig Pearse, the schoolteacher, into a rebel. He delivered the Proclamation of Independence at the Easter Uprising in 1916. The British executed him on May 3rd. Democratic idealists, it is hard to understand why the English made such a hash of it in Ireland.

It was near dusk when Charles and I began our solitary trek toward Conamara. We didn't follow the coast route. We took the main road, N59, which is a little faster unless you are an Irish driver, hoping to make Cashel House in time for dinner. The highway cuts straight through the middle of the peninsula that is western County Galway. For at least half the way it is an ordinary road bordered with scraggly hedgerows, peppered with white single-story houses. It is not until the tiny village of Oughterard that the countryside opens up. The tangled growth which obscures views of the land begins to disappear. A curtain lifts. When you reach Maam Cross, you're in Conamara. It is a magical moment. Each day, each hour of each day, is a study of contrasts, of unlimited space overwhelming the senses with a delirious rush of freedom. Scudding clouds, pools of water, steep-sided mountains, rocky land, sturdy, twisted gorse and low-growing heathers and sun and rain and wind and nothing to stop them.

On this evening our solitary drive was brought to an abrupt halt. What we took to be a lone driver creeping along ahead of us unfurled into a line of cars stretching as far as an eye peering around a side-view mirror could see—fifty vehicles at least, and more likely, more. It was a funeral cortege. We fell in behind, accompanying the unknown body on its melancholy journey through the undulating bog. We left the procession at the turn-off, long miles from Galway town, just this side of Cashel. It was an oddity for me, the sight of a funeral cortege. I had impatiently passed lines of cars, led by the raven-black hearse, slowing traffic on Highway 101 in the Bay Area, poking along as if loath to reach the exiled cemetery far away from the City, banished for all time to the southern peninsula. I had not given them a second thought.

In Conamara, and, perhaps, all over Ireland, the funeral procession is part of the landscape. I see its slow progress to the Ballinafad church or into the Clifden cathedral from my front room window at Derrynavglaun, or, when I am outside gardening. The muffled rumble of a single passing motorist a quarter of a mile from the house disappears, smothered by the sallies and the reeds. Multiplied, the sound swells in volume, sending waves over the quartz and limestone rocks clamoring and clinging up the mountainside. If the mourners are going to the parish church in Ballinafad, I lose sight of them for a minute as they pass behind a hillock, cross the Canal Stage bridge and turn right off the main road. I see them emerge coming to a halt along Ballynahinch lake, cars stopping and parking as near to the church, which I cannot see, as they can get.

Waves of sound are not allowed at Cashel House so Charles and I slept late, waking to the luxury of warm scones and fresh cream at our table overlooking the lovingly tended gardens. We roved a countryside tangled with blackberry brambles and edged with kelp, an embroidery of warm ochre at the edge of the sea. Drifting aimlessly, we chanced on one Matt O'Sullivan, Auctioneer. A tall, immaculately dressed

Conamara man, father of two, or maybe, it was three, sets of twins, we persuaded Matt to spend an afternoon with us checking out property listings.

We looked at several places. One, a brand-new architectural rendering of the traditional Conamara stone cottage, backed onto a small lake. It took my eye immediately. Charles shook his head. A clone sat within hailing distance. Too neighborly. The others, in various states of repair from impossible to a coat of paint will do it, were located in tidy villages of a dozen or so houses. Too many people. We were back in the car as soon as civility would allow.

Derrynavglaun sitting by itself a quarter of a mile down a boreen, nestled in the embrace of the Twelve Bens, was the last place on Matt's list. A gate, halfway up the muddy road, was locked. Off to one side, a car squatted, mired down in the bog. A couple from England, stopping at the locked gate blocking the road midway up to the house, had given up on their attempt to look the place over. Trying to turn around, they went ever so slightly off the packed earth, and that was that. With a little pushing, a little shoving, a little to-ing and fro-ing, Charles and Matt sent them on their way. We left our cars on the road, climbed the gate and made our way through a field of wild daisies and creeping buttercup. Next to the ruins of three stone outbuildings was a tiny cottage. We peeked through the windows. There was a stove and a sink. An open fireplace. The place looked habitable. Not a neighbor in sight. Matt said a French doctor was selling it after a five-year tenure. We probably should have asked why, but instead we contented ourselves with thanking our escort for his time before carefully backing down the road.

Arriving home a few days later, the phone began to ring almost before I unlocked the door. It was Charles already at work on *Sunday Morning* calling to break the big news. He had that very hour sent a check to Matt O'Sullivan. The dollar was strong. Conamara property cheap. Charles found a royalty check from his publisher in the stack of mail piled high on his New York desk. Might as well spend it. Derrynavglaun was ours. For the first time in my life, I was a property owner.

We didn't get back to Ireland until April of the following year. There was a lot more work to be done than we expected. Mother and Charles and I bunked not at Derrynavglaun but at Cashel House while we made our plans. Charles strong-armed J.R. into donating a year of his life to get the place in shape. We would drop by now and then, see how things were going. Supervise. Enjoy ourselves.

J.R. got to work. He tore up the floors or what there was of them, and against all local advice, put in plank flooring. He ripped open the front of the house, found an unemployed German boat builder up in County Mayo to fashion arched teak doors. He thatched the smallest stone cabin, the one which had been a forge when the Mannion brothers owned the place. Mother and I bought stripped pine furniture in Kilkenny and Moss pottery at Thomastown.

Charles fished the Ballynahinch waters with a big, heavy rod used for sea trout and salmon, reluctantly stowing his Winston graphite in the cupboard holding the immersion heater. I mowed the hayfield with a lawn mower becoming an instant source of derision among the surrounding sheep farmers. Mother picked daffodils and tried to get the fireplace to burn without smoking. Bewildered by the enigmas of foreign living, she never resolved to her own satisfaction, why turf, just rectangles of dirt as far as she was concerned, burned at all, or why, when she handed a bank cashier a $100 bill, she only got back £72.

We were at ease at Derrynavglaun. I was dazzled at the very idea of having a cottage in Ireland. To have two acres to play in was almost inconceivable. I undertook massive gardening projects. Mother scoffed at my exertions, pointing out that my great, great, great grandfather had the good sense to abandon the back-breaking labor of rock clearing and emigrate to the States. It was San Francisco Stocks all over again. She preferred to spend her time with Charles.

The two of them explored the low hills and bog surrounding our patch of land, walking hand in hand over to the Glenhoughan creek where she sat on a bank admiring Charles's zinging casts upstream with the reclaimed Winston. The two of them drove into Galway town and bought Elizabeth David's *English Bread and Yeast Cookery* book. They spent afternoons in the kitchen struggling with Ms. David's rigorous historical research and offhand recipes trying to construct a chewy, glutinous loaf, not too heavy but with good body. Pages 235 and 272 are folded neatly in two for ease of reference. Page 235 is a table of equivalent measurements in metric, U.S. and Imperial. Pages 272 and 273 set out instructions and counter-instructions for 'The Grant Loaf', a bread, Ms. David tells us, which 'is now part of English domestic bread-baking history.' Here is the recipe of Mrs. Doris Grant who championed the loaf to hundreds of Englishwomen and might have been a help if she had been in the kitchen with Charles and Mother.

(THE ARC ON 226/3
IS RIGHT SIZE)

ARCHED ~~SIZE~~ SPACE BETWEEN
LIVING ROOM and KITCHEN?

BUT:

NOT THIS!

THIS!

(RAISE CEILING TO MAXIMUM HEIGHT)
?

GLASS DOORS TO BEDROOM SAME AS GLASS WINDOW/DOORS
IN "SUN LOUNGE".

(NOT NECESSARILY
THE CORRECT NUMBER
OF WINDOWS)

DOOR — DOOR

DOORS AND WINDOWS
LOOK THE SAME,
ALL
FLOOR TO CEILING

OR ALL DOORS?

WOOD FLOOR IN 'SUN LOUNGE' (WITH THE
EXPECTATION OF WOOD FLOORS THROUGHOUT, EVENTUALLY)

WOOD FLOOR IN BATH, TOO.

Derrynavglaun drawings

3 lb stone-ground, wholewheat flour, 2 pints water at blood heat, 2 teaspoons salt—slightly more or less, according to taste, 3 rounded teaspoons Barbados sugar, honey or black molasses, 3 level British standard teaspoon measures dried yeast.

Mother loved us all, but she loved Charles best. She pinned his cards on her wall, left his letters on the top of her desk, and framed the score cards he tallied during rambunctious Scrabble games. I am an eager but middling game player. Mother studied and pounced. Charles exuding goodwill was deadly, pulling back only if Mother showed signs of bewilderment. It was during one of these Scrabble games in front of the turf fire that lady luck tipped her hat to me. Behind as always, I drew a 'z'. It was going to make me a killing. I triumphantly laid down 'mizen' on a triple. Charles challenged. 'Two "z's".' I couldn't believe it.

We hadn't been at Derrynavglaun long. There were a few books besides Ms. David's bread book that Charles had snatched during our travels. Niall Fallon's *Fly-fishing for Irish Trout*. (Two copies, one soft cover which we found first and then the hardback discovered further down the road.) David Attenborough's *New Generation Guide—Wild Flowers of Britain and Northern Europe*. Bord Fáilte's *Ireland Guide*. (Two of the same edition when we couldn't remember if we had just looked through the first one or had bought it.) We didn't need a dictionary. We had Charles.

Indignant at Charles' challenge, I knew from experience he never made a mistake in spelling or in grammar, but I also knew this time I was right. He had to be bluffing. Charles

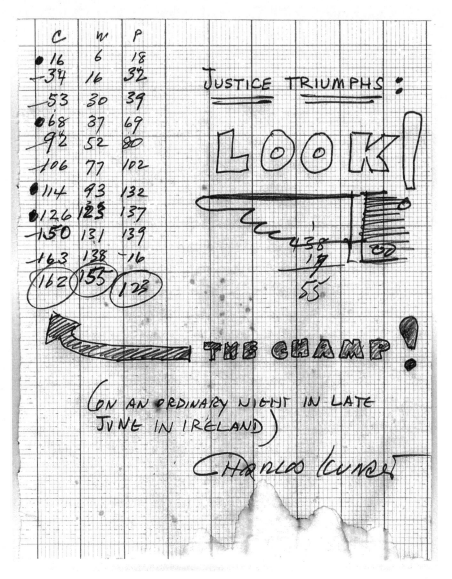

	C	W	P
	● 16	6	18
	34	16	32
	53	30	39
	● 68	37	69
	92	52	80
	106	77	102
	● 114	93	132
	● 126	123	137
	150	131	139
	163	138	16
	162	153	123

JUSTICE TRIUMPHS:

LOOK!

438
19
55

← THE CHAMP!

(ON AN ORDINARY NIGHT IN LATE
JUNE IN IRELAND)

CHARLES KURALT

Scrabble score card

119

was tranquil. 'Two "z's".' I gritted my teeth and surrendered. The next day I drove into Clifden and picked up a paperback *Oxford English Dictionary*. I refer you to page 472, left hand column, first entry: '**mizen** lowest fore-and-aft sail of full-rigged ship's mizen-mast.' This is the scorecard Mother carefully framed and hung on the wall at Derrynavglaun next to Charles' wellies and waders and fly rods and hats from Millar's.

There was a period of an hour at Derrynavglaun, the only hour I can remember that she was not pleasantly besotted by him, when Mother was so mad at Charles she could only hurl abuse at this, her favorite child, her only son. We had gone into Clifden for supplies. It is ten miles of curves and hills bordered by high hedges of rhododendron and fuchsia, a narrow road, tapering into a tendril for a half mile or so when it hairpins around Derrylea, a small lake attractive to anglers. Charles and I fell into a pattern when it came to driving. On any given day I was a faster driver. I chauffeured to and from airports, picking up and delivering. He piddled along on holidays, and, when we were about to miss something, took over, driving faster and surer than I ever would or could. This was a piddling day. I began needling Charles about his unhurried progress along a road I already knew by heart. Shopping bores me, the road bored me. I wanted to get back to my digging and pruning. Charles ignored me until I made the fatal mistake of suggesting that perhaps I should drive. We were just coming up to Derrylea.

Charles downshifted into his 'just watch me' mood, rammed the little Fiat Uno into third and floorboarded it. Mother, weighing less than a hundred pounds, was slung around in the back seat like a bag of turf until she came to rest on the edge of the seat, legs akimbo, clutching her seat belt, tweed hat askew on the side of her head, wrapped in blind fury.

'You fool!' she shouted.

I spoke placatingly. 'Please, Charles. You're frightening Mother.'

Charles's response was to take his eyes off the road long enough to give me a quick glance, a look meant to remind me he was doing the driving.

It wasn't until we were well past Peter McDonagh's neat Conamara-thatched cottage perched on the far shore of Derrylea that Charles' foot lightened on the accelerator. We drove home in silence punctuated by Mother's bursts of rage. As soon as we arrived at Derrynavglaun, Mother went into her room for a nap. I busied myself cutting down leggy berberis bushes to a compact hedge of three-feet at the bottom of the orchard. Charles slowly and methodically sanded off the garish green on the metal entry gate and with delicate, drip-free strokes, repainted it a lustrous black.

Neither Mother nor Charles would have made good ex-pats. Their roots were deep in American soil. Mother frankly did not understand the idea of an hyphenated American. Charles took hope from the fact we were all immigrants at one time or another—even Cherokees and Choctaw had come across a sea or land bridge and now were ipso facto Americans—a to him, glorious melting pot. When his younger brother, Wallace, did a paternal family history traveling to Slovenia videotaping and researching, Charles was interested, but not much. He, himself, did a side story on the Slovenian

Kuralts when he was covering the winter Olympics in Albertville. He came away without any sense of ethnic pride or a hankering to return. Charles' ancestral home was the hardscrabble soil of North Carolina. Mother and Charles hung around uncomfortable waiting rooms at Kennedy International Airport and suffered the tasteless rolls and tepid coffee served on tedious overseas flights to please me. They enjoyed Derrynavglaun while they were there, but they were happy enough to pack their bags once the holiday was over.

Charles who left me messages on pillows and in wreaths left one at Derrynavglaun. It is hard to read, faded, and once mistakenly painted over, but you can still make out the so-familiar hand high on the door jamb of the little front bedroom. 'I love you, Pat.'

Derrynavglaun Diary

FIRST, ME:

Wednesday, August 13, 1987: It started raining sometime after 10 p.m. last night, probably early this morning. At 8:00 a.m. the bog and lower meadow were completely covered and water covered the left corner of the Frenchman's fence over to the fifth post on the right and up one fence post toward the house. At 10:45 a.m. I stood at the right corner fence post in water above my ankles. In the center of the meadow I was, maybe, fifteen feet back from the fence line with the water two or three inches from the top of my wellies. The bog gate was covered with only the top and second railing and one-half space below showing. The fence line following the Glenhoughan river was completely submerged for thirty feet in the area where the fence line dips—this is where C. climbed it to fish. Now at 11:45 a.m. the water has receded back to the fifth fence post from the left and is rapidly moving out. The rain has stopped. Hohum. Patrick Joyce built his clamp on the only finger of land in the bog that was not inundated and our Irishman stopped his planting along the path on the left of meadow exactly where the water came. And, now, the water is rushing, rushing to the sea. At noon the upper meadow is clear; the bog gate probably uncovered; I can see the top, first and second rungs and a great space below. Someone taller, that is with taller wellies, could walk the road to the gate.

NOW, CHARLES:

Thursday Aug 20 1987—Flood occurred again—just as before. (Wed. afternoon, Sean King and Paddy John Joyce were agreeing, in the bar of the Ballynahinch hotel, that the flood was one in 21 years. This makes two in 21 years.) Water rose higher than before—peaked about 10:30 a.m., was down by about noon. Peak was 4 inches below top of bracing beam in SE corner fence post. There was a steady bubbling of water for more than a day afterwards from middle of a doorway wall in shed—obvious underground stream—flooding walkway to gate.

Sat Aug 22 '87. River now down way below its banks! Can be waded in places with water no higher than ankles. Painted main gate black. Planted Corsican mint beneath wall across from gatehouse; 2 Campanula beneath wall across from turf shed; basil in herb garden; and (homage to Vita Sackville-West) clematis Montana Rubens above stone wall on east side of back yard. (P. cut down old hydrangea to make room for the clematis.) J.R. thinned ugly ('palmetto.') P. pruning to open views to orchard, hills and village of Derrynavlaghn [*sic*].

Criss-crossing America with the crew, Charles discovered the trout streams of Montana. That was before the state became a destination for those our friend, Ken Ryder, calls cappuccino cowboys. The locals held no truck with passive aggression and disgust was registered by a pithy 'Oh, piss on it.' Outside of Yellowstone, we rarely met another fisherman. We waved farewell to the Sierras where the pristine meadows were beginning to resemble RV parks. Goodbye, Tahoe. Goodbye, Little Truckee, Jack's Canyon, Hot Creek. Hello, Rockies.

We looked around a bit before settling down in southwest Montana wandering up the coast of Oregon and into the hinterlands to stay a while at Sun River in the middle of the state. Nice. Big resort dining room, fireplace in the cabin, lots of canoeing, not much fishing. One foray launched out of Denver's Brown Palace sent us meandering through Wyoming, where we stopped and took photos of a local parade before fishing the creeks of the Medicine Bow Mountain Range. Over every summit a field of wild flowers waited for us on the lower hillsides. Charles pulled over and stopped by a gurgling stream, unloaded our lunch and his fishing gear, spreading a blanket for me to sit on under a large fir. He arranged our lunch of salami and cheese on the red and white checkered cloth and busied himself opening a bottle of wine.

'What's that?' he asked, giving a casual nod with his head.

'What?'

'There at the edge of the blanket.'

I looked down and saw the tip of something shiny poking out of a mat of slender, browning needles.

'It's a piece of foil.'

'See what it is.'

I brushed off the needles, scraped off a bit of dirt and pulled out a square packet. It was foil of some sort, dark chocolate in color lined in silver, folded and held together by a large metal paper clip. I slipped off the clip and unfolded the foil. Inside was a love note. Charles hid it when he and the On The Road crew had rolled by the previous week, stopping for a moment to capture the magnificent view of the valley below. It was Charles taking your heart by surprise.

If a phantom emerged from the shadows of my mind, Charles could sense its attendance almost before I did. When I turned forty he sent me a card, an exuberant Capricorn goat. December 22 to January 19. 'Cool, clever Capricorn becomes more physically attractive as each year passes; often finds greatest acclaim after 40.' He signed it 'C' and added '… yes, but really!' About that time one of the newsweeklies ran a photo spread on major American artists toward the end of their lives, revealing the beauty of women in old age. Who, I asked Charles, do I want to look like when I grow old? Each woman exhibited a riveting presence, each was immensely appealing. I pondered awhile before settling on Louise Nevelson. The stunning portrait of this American sculptor from Kiev, hair invisible under a sleek turban, dramatic make-up, exotic, aloof, was as mysterious as the rhythmic abstract art she constructed. 'No,' Charles shook his head, 'not her.' He pointed to the brown, leathery face of Georgia O'Keefe, strong and clear as her paintings of the desert Southwest. 'Her.'

One of our rambles took us through Glacier National Park up by the Canadian border. Spectacular is understatement when you try to describe the sheer precipices and waterfalls of Montana's glacial Shangra-La. We went back the next year to camp at the edge of the wilderness on the west side of the Continental Divide. The people at the Polebridge store rented us a cabin up the end of a dirt track, one room with a rickety ladder leading to a quilt-filled loft. Light sifted through the calico curtains pouring out stained-glass colors on a plank floor. In the evening we read by the flickering flame of a gas lamp. The old coal stove took the chill off the air in the morning and heated water for bathing. Charles baked a hazelnut cheese cake in its remarkably efficient oven. He had torn the recipe out of a newspaper and was determined to make it for dessert, energetically pounding the resisting hazelnut shells with a hammer to get at the nutmeats. He then ground with an assortment of tools plucked from his fishing bag, the kitchen cabinet and a tool box.

Days were spent on the river, Charles delivering long, swooping casts to a feeding fish or sitting on the bank, sucking M&Ms, watching for rises. At dusk we wound our way back to the cabin, stopping now and again to add to one more violet aster to the bouquet that would grace our dinner table. Our path crossed that of a brown bear and her two cubs one evening. We each suffered a moment of hesitation before mama sent the children into a grove of trees. Hoping to avoid another awkward encounter, Charles sang *On the*

Road to Mandalay whenever we were on a trail, a warning that we were on our way. It was the only song, he said, he could sing on key.

We were a hopeful Adam and Eve in the garden. Again the fishing wasn't so hot.

The following year, Boo Lichtenberg, a Southern charmer turned rancher's wife, inserted a few lines in a fishing magazine's classified section: 'Field house for rent on Montana river.' Bait to a rising trout. That September we flew into Butte, rented a 4-wheel drive, and drove over the Continental Divide to Twin Bridges. The ramshackle house wasn't much, a couple of rooms with faded linoleum and creaky twin beds. It looked like it had been dropped in the middle of its rough hay field by a spent tornado. We hadn't come for the accommodations. We had come for the fishing. A short walk between grazing cattle and over an irrigation ditch landed you on the banks of the Big Hole River. Browns, a few Rainbow. Dry flies. Catch and release. Well. Mostly.

Delbrook Lichtenberg was a cattleman who branded his calves with the Lazy 3 Hanging J, rounded up his steers on horseback, and served you tumblers of whiskey while he tended steaks thrown into the coals of a campfire, searing briefly, before passing around. Delbrook peddled the whole spread not long ago. Said he got tired of losing money. The new owners brought in an architect to neaten the place up, make it look more like a Western ranch. Planted flowers between the steps, cut blocks of sod for a new roof, graveled a sweeping drive. Even kept a cow or two. Looks real pretty.

For twenty-two years beginning the fall of 1976, for the month of September, the Big Hole was ours. A bit of it

(*Above*) Mother and Daddy in Reno, 1943

J.R., Shannon and Kathleen, Easter 1962

First spring with Charles – Shannon, Kathleen and J.R., 1969

Charles at bat, 1969

Charles eating, me brooding, 1970

Charles fishing Hot Creek, 1970

Me sitting at Hot Creek meadow, 1970

Lazy day at Belvedere, 1971

Charles and me, 1971

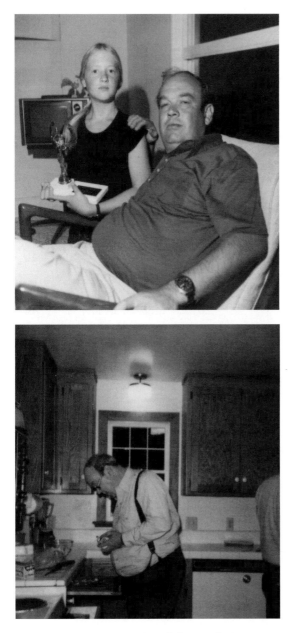

(*Top left*) Awards Ceremony
(*Bottom left*) Beef Bourguignon in the making
(*Right*) Four shots of Charles hamming it up, 1972

A ritual, 1976

(*Above*) Shannon and J.R. at Tahoe, 1978
(*Left*) Kathleen at Belvedere, 1979

Charles peeking down from loft, at me in a cabin kitchen, 1982

Scattering Douglas' ashes, 1985

A small catch at Derrynavglaun, 1987

Mother at Derrynavglaun, 1987

Oslo, 1987

(*Left*) Charles and J.R. at the cabin, 1989

(*Below*) Shannon and Robley, Christmas at the cabin, 1988

(*Left*) The St. John, 1992

(*Below*) Derrynavglaun summer, 1991

Quick snap by J.R., 1993

Kathleen's Graduation from law school, 1994

actually became ours when, nine years after Charles reached down his net to land his first Big Hole trout, he sent me tramping from the field house up the road with a mission. My job was to persuade Boo to persuade Delbrook to sell us some land. Over the years, Delbrook had repeatedly pushed aside Charles' tentative offers to buy. Nope, not an acre. Never. Pleading with Boo to intercede on our behalf, I was as eloquent as I knew how to be. No one would know we were there, I assured her, we would be as elusive as the retiring whitetails, keeping hidden in the willows and the tall grasses. For thirteen years we were as good as our word.

Delbrook and Boo sold us the penultimate parcel on the ranch, a rough triangle, sage and cattails, marsh and willow bordering the river. Like the liege of old, we were given guardianship not just of the land but of the inhabitants as well. Hard-shelled turtles sunning on a shattered log in the creek fell under our protection, as did the porcupine clambering up the cottonwood trunk out of harm's way. We lay claim to the elegant black and white skunk padding along the river's edge, the muskrat burrowing under a weir of reeds, and the beavers pitting their determination to build dams against our resolve to keep one or two trees standing. We threw apples to the deer, marveled at the well-traveled moose, spent hours identifying whatever flew or perched. We made a pact. We would protect these shy, wild creatures. This speck of land would be their sanctuary.

Our section of the Big Hole is a part of Jefferson's Louisiana Purchase. Lewis and Clark mapped the land, traveling up the Jefferson River, to where it forks at what is now Twin Bridges. The northerly fork, which Lewis personally named Wisdom River ('the bold rapid an [d] clear stream Wisdom), is the Big Hole. George Shannon was a private with the party.

[Clark] August 9th Friday 1805—a fine morning wind from the N.E. we proceeded on verry well rapid places more noumerous than below, Shannon the man whome we lost on Wisdom River Joined us, haveing returned to the forks & prosued us up after prosueing Wisdom River one day.

The Journal of Lewis and Clark

Charles calculated George Shannon may have actually camped across the river from the schoolhouse bluff the night he spent on Clark's Wisdom, our Big Hole. I doubt the Private is a limb on our family tree, but Charles and I always pretended he was. He would certainly add a little luster to the crusty old trunk, admired as he was, and trusted, by Lewis and Clark despite an embarrassing inability to keep to the trail.

Charles built his little North Carolina cabin on the Big Hole, hauling in squared-off logs, shrugging off the vicissitudes of supervising from a distance, dropping by for an hour or so whenever he could. We commissioned a San Francisco architect to draw up the plans. When we arrived at his office for our first consultation, Charles was carrying a sketch of the cabin with him, front and side views, and floor plan: six hundred square feet including two porches, front and back, running the entire length of the building. Two rooms and a closed loft for storage. Big stone fireplace.

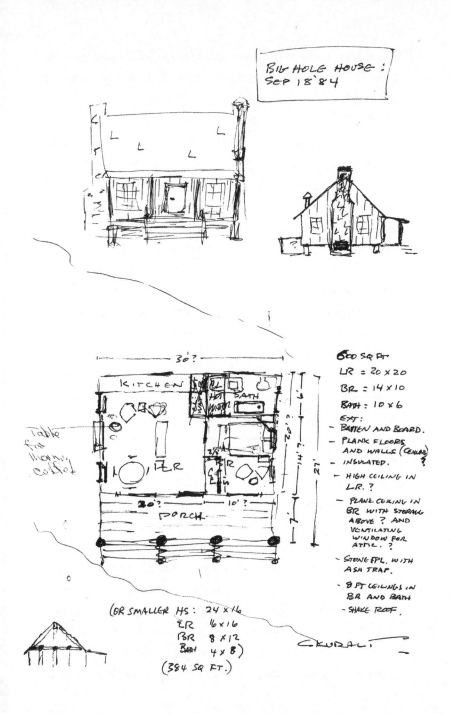

BIG HOLE HOUSE:
SEP 18 '84

600 SQ FT
LR = 20 X 20
BR = 14 X 10
BATH = 10 X 6
EXT:
- BATTEN AND BOARD.
- PLANK FLOORS
  AND WALLS (CEILING)
- INSULATED.
- HIGH CEILING IN
  LR. ?
- PLANK CEILING IN
  BR WITH STORAGE
  ABOVE ? AND
  VENTILATING
  WINDOW FOR
  ATTIC. ?
- STONE FPL. WITH
  ASH TRAP.
- 8 FT CEILINGS IN
  BR AND BATH
- SHAKE ROOF.

KITCHEN
HOT WATER
BATH
Table for hanging coffet
LR
BR
PORCH

30'?
27'
20'?
10'?

(OR SMALLER HS: 24 X 16
   LR   16 X 16
   BR   8 X 12
   BATH 4 X 8)
   (384 SQ FT.)

CKURAL:

I pictured nooks and crannies for a dishwasher, washer and dryer, vacuum cleaner, ironing board, maybe a second half-bath. The architect, a seasoned professional, never blinked. The steep-pitched roof is not as steep as either Charles or the architect envisioned, daylight sneaks under the warped doors, winds rush up a hollow wall driving blasts of cold air into a drafty bath. Uncertain workmanship and questionable charges didn't bother Charles. He was safe here, he said. When he was away he could sound down-right plaintive counting the days until he could get back.

There was one change in the original drawing. Charles and J.R. stopped by for an afternoon visit after the loft was finished. Shut off from the main room by a plank wall it had become a cozy second bedroom with two low windows facing the bluff downstream. The cabin plans yielded not a foot of spare space for a staircase so a pull-down ladder was fitted into the bedroom ceiling. J.R. watched in dismay as the sturdy ladder unfolded, a mighty slash across the foot of the bed. He looked at Charles. Charles looked thoughtful. The identical picture had flashed through their minds. J.R. sneaking into the bedroom like a thief in the night, and, ever so quietly, lowering his bedroom steps preparing to ascend over the heads of the couple sleeping below. Maybe, Charles murmured, this wasn't such a good idea after all. The upshot of it was a set of slats flush against the hall wall ascending ladderlike up through a two-foot square opening in the floor of the loft. The plank wall divider was replaced by an open wainscoting through which bounding reflections of the fire play hide and seek.

The slat ladder works fine for the kids. Roberta didn't have any trouble with it. It was a bit of a trial for Mother.

When she and I were alone, I slept in the loft. She drifted off to sleep in the glow of the bedroom fireplace. When Charles, Mother and I were at the cabin together, Mother braved the climb with Charles handing her up in his courtly fashion, a routine Mother thoroughly enjoyed. Most often Charles and I were alone on the Big Hole. He hadn't planned on visitors other than the family. That plan never changed. The caretakers might drop in for a chat. If there were problems on the river, Charles would invite a commissioner or two to sort it out. That was about it. If he was feeling particularly threatened, Charles kept the Burma Road gate locked. Other times we just threw a wire loop over the post to keep it closed.

Life on the Big Hole was as sweet as it gets. We read, wrote, walked, talked, fished, cooked. In fact we cooked almost as much as we fished. The recipes were simple, stews, *linguine* with clam sauce, whatever you could pick up at Mac's, our local emporium. When Charles and I began cooking together in the Sixties, our culinary enthusiasms far out-distanced the equipment in our kitchen. We expanded haphazardly buying whatever was needed for that night's dinner and not a soupcon more. We headed to China Town after a dinner of sweet and sour pork on crackling rice at San Francisco's Mandarin Restaurant to pick up a wok, basket steamer and flat wire spoon. I place the blame for a growling automatic pasta maker firmly on the shoulders of a North Beach *trattoria* which, without fanfare, served us fresh *fettuccine* studded with buttery morels. Julia Child's kitchen was the inspiration for a sturdy iron rack above the gas stove on which we hung a set of heavy copper pots, relegating to Derrynavglaun my copper-bottomed Revereware. I had painstakingly collected it during the lean years by sending in coupons cut from Kraft Macaroni and Cheese cartons plus a dollar.

Shifting operations to a two-room cabin called for down-sizing. The antique cabinet we hung on the wall next to the sink couldn't begin to hold a kitchen collection almost twenty years in the making. We tried not to think about the gastronomic no-man's land stretching before us as we parceled out hinged pate molds and balloon whisks to our flock of fledgling cooks. It was something of a shock when after a few weeks of trial and error, we learned what Mother had always known. All we needed to turn out a satisfying meal was a sturdy butcher block, a sharp knife or two and a camp cook assortment of iron skillets and stewpots.

One dish took the blue ribbon. We discovered it in Montana. It was the Cornish pasty. When Charles and I first began flying into Butte, mom and pop restaurants were dishing out the tasty meat pies as casually as the chains throw you a hamburger today. How the pasty got to Butte is an interesting bit of history. At the turn of the century, Butte's copper mines attracted immigrants from all over the world including the Cornish miners who lost their jobs when Cornwall tin mines lost their battle to the encroaching sea. The Copper Capital's early diversity is reflected in a 1976 edition of *Butte's Heritage Cookbook* which J.R. rescued from a used book shop and presented to us. In addition to the seven different pasty recipes, there are instructions for preparing Serbian *Klenedljine Od Sliv* (Plum Dumplings), Swedish *Kalvsylta* (Jellied Veal) and Lebanese *Mjadra* (Lentil Pottage). Butte was Charles's melting pot in spades.

The Irish and Welsh also lay claim to the pasty (pro-nounced *pass-tee*), but Butte gives the nod to the Cornish. The Cornishmen's 'letter from 'ome'—meat and potatoes wrapped in a pastry sized to fit a miner's pocket—was a staple in the Butte mines. If the pastry was a little tough, it had to be, just like the men who carried it.

The signal at the cabin that dinner was about to be prepared was Charles's request for an apron. A bibbed apron to be exact. While the precise apron varied over the years, it was as often as not the twill job, blue and white striped with red grosgrain ties at the waist and neck. There was a white apron with red checks bearing the exotic label, PARIS HALLES VILLETTE, a leftover from San Francisco Stocks which made an understudy appearance on days the twill was in the laundry. The final choice on the closet shelf was a cheerful, but small, cream-colored apron with appliquéed red and yellow blanket flowers, blue lupines and bright daisies, a gift from the National Wildflower Research Center in Austin, Texas. Subjected to frequent examination to see if it might possibly have altered in size, the apron was, time and again, reluctantly placed back on the shelf once Charles had reassured himself, it, unlike himself, had not grown at all.

To Charles, cooking meant slicing and dicing. The one item we lugged up to the cabin from Marin was a maple chopping block. A solid 24" × 30" × 12" with an overall height of 34", it was crafted for the serious cook. Charles arranged on the block's broad surface, as if for a portrait, potatoes, turnips, carrots, button mushrooms, a yellow onion and two or three cloves of garlic, stepped back, pondered a moment, and, invariably, added a sprig of parsley for color. After sharpening a butcher knife on a 12" steel, he set to work. Mushrooms were quartered, the onion diced, the garlic minced. He cubed the steak though Cornishwomen insist the meat should be sliced. The size of the cube depended upon Charles' estimate of the tenderness of the steak he had grabbed out of Mac's freezer. Everything went into a crockery bowl. He shook bottles of Tabasco and Worcestershire over the mixture until he figured it was enough, added salt and pepper and gave the mixture a toss or two. Done.

Ignoring tradition, I made the pastry in a food processor, so it was already chilling in the refrigerator by the time he was ready for it. Charles used a pie plate bottom and a paring knife to cut out circles of dough, heaping them with filling. He folded the dough and crimped the edges with an artistic flourish before sliding the pasties onto a battered metal cookie sheet and shoving them into the oven.

While this was going on, I set the table. The cabin dishes are JugTown pottery from North Carolina, a gray clay tempered with brown, decorated with a single stem of delicately painted blue flowers. We rarely used a tablecloth, opting instead for heavy blue and white woven placemats which mimic tiny rag rugs. Charles arranged the flowers, a bouquet of misty flax or pungent sage, in a cut-glass jar.

When the pasties were done, Charles dribbled a bit of boiling beef stock into a vent in the top of the crust, garnishing the golden crescents with a dollop of sour cream. I carried the plates to the table. He lit the candles, poured the wine, raised his glass, smiling, for the ritual toast.

'Ain't we livin'!'

Delbrook Lichtenberg found it less painful to part with a few acres of ranch land than he imagined. He named his price, no quibbling, and as part of the bargain continued to run his cattle on the property. That proved such a good deal, he sold us two more parcels, one on each side of the cabin, fifty acres on the arid bluff at the extreme end of the ranch and a lush forty acre section on the river upstream. Charles lusted for the river frontage. The bluff was the trade off. We accepted it as a barricade against development. We came to change our minds about that because of the Pageville schoolhouse. Sitting next to the highway just before the turn-off to the cabin, the school, built in the 1880s, had been closed for decades. Maundering cows found a smidgen of protection in it during the winter when Canadian cold fronts swoop down dropping the temperature into the minus twenties. The old building had become a fusion of manure and rotting boards To us this seemed not only unjust, but a terrible waste. The West is filled with natural splendors, but there is precious little in modern building to delight the eye.

We moved the schoolhouse to the bluff where it overlooks the river and the cabin. Ken Ryder and Jerry Tollefson spent a year renovating it, exactly as it was outside, graying boards and carpenter gothic. Inside, all teak and mahogany and marble. It was to be Charles's study, his place to retire. We stumbled onto Ken and Jerry quite by accident. They were a serendipitous find.

Shannon was finishing her undergraduate degree at Mills College in Oakland. Her major was European history. Her advisor was a natty, tough-minded Italian who, I suspect, found her a little breezy for his taste. It had been a rough semester. Shannon was casting about for a way to improve the situation. Her approach, almost always, is to try to charm a problem away. Following this line of attack, she signed on as a volunteer for one of the professor's pet projects, restoring Oakland to the beautiful city it had been at the turn of the century. An urban fair was planned for the gardens behind one of the grand old Victorian homes which somehow managed to survive skirmishes with blight, earthquakes and developers. Shannon would be in attendance. So, as it turned out, would I. My daughter reasoned if one charmer was good, two were better and strong-armed me into putting in an appearance.

I moseyed along gravel paths, stopping at one booth or another in an attempt to be winsome. When I arrived at one stall, the woman noted for her expertise in renovating old houses was taking a tea break . Having hoped I might obtain something practical from this exercise, like an idea or two for the schoolhouse, I was sorely disappointed. The old building was resting precariously on the bluff. That was as far as it went. Charles and I were in our research stage. Books and magazines were scattered over all the cabin's flat surfaces. Charles read. I winced. Writers lingered lovingly over the difficulties of restoration citing nervous breakdowns and

general mayhem as possible outcomes to any serious under-
taking. After talking to the people manning the booths at the
Oakland fair, I was beginning to believe those writers had
minimized the problems we were facing.

Missing my moment with Oakland's resident restoration
guru, not knowing what else to do, I began chatting up the
young woman smiling apologetically at me from behind the
make-shift counter. A discussion of old versus new, tawdry
versus genuine, gradually lost its theoretical airiness. Beginning
an unhurried descent over the Rocky Mountains, our
reflections at last touched down precisely in the center of
Bozeman, Montana. My agreeable interlocutor's brother-in-
law, a man who devoted himself to building restoration,
lived and worked one hundred straight-arrow miles from the
cabin, a two hour drive for Charles and me in the Jeep, an
hour and a half for Ken in his Saab.

Ken Ryder, son of a United Nations diplomat, turned
down life in the fast lane. Opting to raise his family in the
'last, best place', Ken brought a good eye, a steady hand and
his familiarity with the art worlds of Italy and New York
with him when he began work on the schoolhouse. He also
brought Jerry Tollefson, another son of, this time a newspaper
editor, who wanted a quieter life than his father had known.
The two men became acquainted while they were attending
the University of Colorado. Their friendship was set in
concrete during the year they spent commuting from Bozeman
to the schoolhouse.

With two master craftsman at work, Charles and I
sprang into action. We began shopping. The cabin is an
eclectic mix of styles gathered higgledy-piggledy during flight

delays, On The Road travels and lightening assaults on Marin's colorful shopping bazaar. We found on San Anselmo's furniture row a folding French wine-tasting table and two chairs so small and fragile no one dares sit on them. Charles grabbed an armful of Navajo rugs when he had an afternoon to kill in New Mexico. The round dining table was shipped from a North Carolina craft fair. I found the four Shaker dining chairs in a little shop in Inverness.

Charles and I agreed this wouldn't do for the schoolhouse. A fishing cabin is one thing. An elegant, gentleman's library is quite another. We headed for New York with its fabled salvage shops. Squirming between carved wood panels, wiggling around heaps of cornices, capitols and caryatids, climbing fortresses of masonry, we found treasures we had only imagined. We said yes at once to an ornate double door with leaded glass and brass fittings for the entrance hall. The door's scrollwork later found an echo in Jerry and Ken's hand-crafted fireplace surround. To provide a hint as to what might lay behind the schoolhouse's plain front door, we wanted to inset a narrow, leaded glass panel in the wall directly above it, a clue for the discerning. Unable to settle on which leaded pane to inset, we put off the decision until it could be made in situ and sent two home. The debate over the practicality of an Art Deco elevator cage continued for several weeks before Charles sounded the death knell declaring an elevator, even, and most especially, a one-story elevator, pretentious. I often wish we had taken the elevator when we had the chance. The steep mahogany staircase with its broad landing is eye-catching but it has no history. A massive partner's desk located in one of London's musty antique shops softened the newness of the steps recasting their role in the room. Charles brought back an ethereal yellow silk rug from China for a planned reading corner. I wanted his portrait to hang over the fireplace. Charles declined, deeming the gesture self-aggrandizing. Ignoring my earnest protests, he commissioned Russell Chatham, an exile from Marin, to paint a portrait of a river, our river, if possible, as a tribute to our last wilderness.

Ken and Jerry always had a list of questions on the schoolhouse construction when we were lucky enough to spend a few days at the cabin. Should the fireplace marble be green or brown? Would we put Mexican or Portuguese tile in the bath? Did we need an oven in the tiny kitchen or would a microwave do? The last major decision had to do with the bluff itself. Should it be left as it was, or dare we challenge nature with a plant or two? We weren't sure whether we should chalk up the barrenness of the mesa to Delbrook's bulls or to the soil itself. The surrounding vegetation is as simple and restrained in manner as a high-country cowboy. The hills are dappled with buckbrush and scrub pine. Low growing bitterroot, hugs the dry, rocky soil, heralding the Big Hole spring with fragile pale pink blossoms. Subdued most of the year, spiny plains cactus, our prickly pear, calls brief attention to itself in the early summer with waxy yellow blooms. In late summer fragrant gray-green sagebrush offers clusters of tiny silver flowerlets to attentive walkers. It is a muted landscape made lovely by the changing waters and frequent dazzling sun. Maybe, some of that growth would find its way back to the schoolhouse once the bulls found another place to winter. Maybe, the best plan was to sit back and see what happened.

Unlike the schoolhouse solitary on the bluff, the cabin sits down in the bottom, the narrow, fertile strip bordering the river. Tall, weathered cottonwoods spread canopies of shade, and shrubby willows form dense thickets in the hollows and along our creek adding shadowy depth to an essentially level landscape. The meadow grasses are a mix of alfalfa, rye, barley and wild iris. It is about as close to heaven as a dry fly fisherman can get. We had tried improving on nature our first spring at the cabin with a monumental lack of success

The land inside the split rail fence had been laid bare by the building process. The soft grasses were gone, fossilized by repeated violations of bulldozers and cranes. A thin layer of earth barely disguised the rocky hardpan underneath. We thought a field of wild flowers would be nice, better even than the grass. We assumed, since they were wild, the blossoms we tenderly gathered over the years during walks and wanderings would arrive by the thousands in response to our eager invitation thus saving us from the drudgery of double-digging and the complexities of plant nutrition. On one of our trips I landed at Bozeman's Gallatin Field carrying a load of optimism and a suitcase crammed with five pound bags of seed: poppies, bachelor buttons, blue flax, whatever the experts said would grow in the Rocky Mountains. Arriving a few hours ahead of me, Charles, equally sanguine, loaded the back of the Jeep with sacks of fertilizer, sturdy wooden-handled rakes and a mile of garden hose. Before breakfast the next morning, he was hard at it scratching at the ground around the cabin with his brand new rake. I joined him after clearing away the breakfast dishes. The work required more muscle than either of us expected. I quit almost immediately. Charles was not deterred. Flushed, sweat dripping from his forehead, he incised broad swaths from drive to river, shouting for more seed after each lap, casting feathery grains in broad arcs with bacchanalian abandon. I sat on the porch watching the birds swoop down behind him, gorging themselves on the unexpected feast of wildflower seed.

There has never been a field of wildflowers at the cabin. A year or two after the assault of the builders, the wild rose bushes made a heroic comeback. They spill over the rail fence forming a natural hedge and have sent up a shoot or two to peep into the cabin windows. A couple of gooseberry bushes, which Charles would have done away with but couldn't, have threaded their way through the front steps in stunning designer fashion. We contented ourselves with mowing a clearing around the cabin in the recovered grasses with a path cut through to the upriver gate. It was all we ever needed.

We did plant a meadow of wild flowers at the schoolhouse and a grove of aspen trees, and put in a sprinkling system to make sure the wildflowers and aspen survived. The schoolhouse is lovely rising above that garland of rippling color, but it is the cabin that is full of life. In the evenings the wild creatures show themselves, venturing out of their secret places to pay a visit. Charles and I each had a favorite. Mine was, is, the tiny spotted fawn leaping and jumping in a frenzy of delight. Charles took a particular fancy to the Ring-necked pheasant, so full of himself, strutting across the yard. To entice the royal courtier to stay close to us, he put two feed boxes in the yard, one by the shed, the other on the river bank. He filled the boxes twice a day with cracked corn and carefully charted the comings and goings. He noted when the birds arrived late at mid-morning rather than making their customary appearance shortly after sunrise, full of worry that the coyote who had thrilled us with his mournful cries the night before might have had more than music on his mind.

The feed boxes proved a trial. The raccoons turned them over. Whitetail deer sparred with the pheasants for pride of place. On their own initiative the boxes began to edge away from their original locations, hiding in the grass or sliding toward the river. When one box vanished completely, Charles stashed the second in the shed. We took to scattering a line of corn across the edge of the clearing. This open invitation to come and dine proved a success. Within twenty-four hours the word was out. Demand increased the length of the feed line until it stretched across a quarter of the clearing. At dusk we sat on the front steps watching the tawny whitetail doe and her sweet fawn, our lame raccoon, an elegantly striped black and white skunk, the timid porcupine, a dumb bunny or two and the gaily-colored cock pheasant and his harem calmly supping, forgetting for the moment the friction between man and beast.

When we were not around to feed them, the animals kindly house-sat for us, dining a la carte on the willows and dandelions, burrowing in under a fallen tree for a nap or bedding down in the tall grass by the split-rail fence. We were happy to know they were around when we were not. Happier still at the first glimpse of their startled expressions captured in the beam of our headlights when we arrived late at night, glad to be back.

11–3–87 Dear Pat, … I went over to 'the ranch' yesterday and looked over the job … the structural integrity of the building is excellent. More than anything else this is a testimonial to the builder. He was obviously a professional who took pride in his work … Sincerely, Ken

1–11–88 Dear Pat, … When you & Charles were here the last time, Charles mentioned to me he would like to locate a bell to install in the cupola. Last week an oldtimer stopped by the job who lives on the Burma Road about 4–5 miles upriver from your place. In any case he claims to have attended the school back in 1912 when he was 6 years old. He certainly had some interesting & colorful stories to tell about the schoolhouse & the history of the local area. He also claims to have an old bell lying in his yard that we may be able to acquire—I'll look into this matter … Sincerely, Ken

2–8–88 Dear Pat, … I am in the process of drawing a sketch of the river side of the building with some ideas for doors, arched windows, etc. … Sincerely, Ken

2–14–88 Dear Pat, … I have … enclosed a drawing of the rear (east) elevation … It is the lay-out that Charles expressed to me as one he favors most strongly. I am interested in both your & Charles' (*sic*) thoughts on this particular design … The particular type(s) of doors is a decision that you and Charles will have to make … We … begin work on the fancy-pattern shingles (the rounds & diamonds) which go under the eaves … Sincerely, Ken

4-26-88 Dear Pat, … Jerry & I are amassing brochures, etc. on various types of stair details, wood-paneling systems, etc. and also have additional material for your perusal when you come in May. The weather is wild!—We had a major spring storm the past 2 days, with up to two feet of heavy, wet snow in the mountains—good for the watersheds— today the sun is breaking through. Give our best to Charles … Sincerely, Ken

P.S. We saw a turkey on your land last week, along the slough!

CABIN DIARY, 1988

September 15, 1988

Woke to see two fawns walking about feeder, nosing toward a hen pheasant who walked in circles, one fawn or the other just behind her. A most unusual slow dance of young deer and bird!

Walked about yard to find few wildflowers blooming: a bit of yarrow and showy flowers with deep red at center and bright yellow at tips of petals. Still enough to fill a vase when added tall dandelion-like flowers from edge of willow thickets. In some places where Beverly had the weeds pulled, only bare ground remains. The wildflowers are a

(blanket-flower)

puzzlement! We have two more expensive bags of them. I know better than to think I can merely plant them and they'll flourish.

Walked through field and marsh, beautiful views of schoolhouse from cattails along creek, and climbed hill to schoolhouse. P. climbed through window to let us in. Very satisfying! Deck is finished and fits as well as we could have hoped. The walk offered pretty views of our 100 acres, river and network of creeks. From up there, it's clear why the place is so beloved by deer, cranes and pheasants.

Came back to watch swallows feeding chirping young in nest above front porch. Deer in yard, including, toward evening, last month's doe and two fawns. A skunk, vivid black and white, scurried through yard, humping along after sundown.

The river is the lowest I've ever seen it. Rises the length of it in the morning. The wind came up in the afternoon. All of Montana was closed to hunting, fishing, camping and even hiking for a few days because of the danger of wildfires. Fires have been burning all summer, which has been memorably, historically, hot and dry. But there was snow and rain four days ago and the order is lifted. Still the Big Hole will be closed to fishing Oct 1 to allow the brown trout to spawn in the shallow water unmolested.

Today was warm at midday, high clouds. Down to about 38° last night. Fires tonight in both fireplaces.

A triumph with the FM antenna tacked up, we receive WRIC-FM (*sic*) via the Dillon translator—music fills the house! 105.5!

September 14, 1988—Warmer, though still quite cool at night. Many rises in morning, more sporadic in afternoon. Water in river very low. Fished for 2 hours 12:30–2:30. One whitefish, then a 14-in rainbow, then another whitefish, all downstream from house, all on yellow Goofus Bug #16 or so. Killed the trout for dinner—only to be told by Delmar in evening that river is catch-and-release until it closes to fishing Oct. I. So—my first *poached*, fried trout.

Heron flying low along river. Golden eagle flying high above house.

September 15, 1988—Lovely cloudless day. Wildflowers picked 2 days ago mostly survived until tonight, a pretty bouquet in glass for on table. New flowers have bloomed here and there—enough to replenish the jar tomorrow.

P. cooked wonderful cracked wheat braided loaf! I— with much clumsy difficulty—mounted FM antenna in loft and cleaned up bookcase. P. vacuumed. The living room tidy and neat.

Porcupine crossed bridge before sundown. A whitetail deer circled where corn and wheat feeder was across creek (until I moved it this morning.) Heron flying upstream.

Toyed with new laptop computer. Tomorrow I will spend time trying to make it work. Then I hope to do a bit of serious writing each day to impress Neil Nyren who looms in the future like the Angel of Death. Very hard to take him seriously after a lovely day like this.

Last night we read a James Joyce short story. The night before, one by Stephen Crane. Tonight—?

September 16, 1988—(We read James Thurber's *The Catbird Seat* and a story about a priest and his housekeeper by J.F. Powers.)

P. went to the Sallere's nursery at Whitehall and came back with Shasta daisies, delphiniums and lavender to be planted. She heard of a landscaper at Cardwell who might be the man to work at schoolhouse. We have the idea of a grove of aspens up there.

I ignorantly erased Word Perfect from the computer in an effort to clean the memory for my own files!

Walked down to old creeks upstream to find them without water except for stagnant pools, and many beaver-felled trees fallen across and beside them. On the walk home, with wet feet from having stepped off stepping stones at one place, I pondered the trouble and cost of having the creeks cleaned up. Surprised an owl and a heron in creek bed and returned to find five or six whitetail deer at edge of front yard.

Read Delmore Schwarz with fire crackling.

September 17, 1988—Drove to Bozeman to have writing program restored to computer by a bemused young genius named Peter Bennett at Computerland shop. On the way back down Burma Road, photographed group of mule deer in meadow below, all staring at camera with mule ears raised.

Deer and two fawns were at gate of fence in back yard when I went out for wood. A strong cold wind from the north. Cooked a stew for Ken and Jerry, who are sleeping in their bags at the schoolhouse for want of rooms in town. As they left, a wet snow began.

September 18, 1988—The snow dusted the grass, the shed roof and the top of the fence and brush pile. It had melted away by 10 a.m. except on the dry hills and distant mountains. The overcast day turned bright and cold.

Walked in late afternoon to the field house and back in a loop to east. Saw no turkeys but treed a porcupine and surprised a buck mule deer with handsome antlers, and his harem across a field. Downy woodpecker, ducks flying high, hornet's nest. Rabbit at riverside spied through bathroom window. A baby. He spied us, too. Also saw a dark cat-like animal running in distance. Delmer says bobcat, lynx or wolverine.

September 19, 1988—Cold overcast morning after a night in 20's. P. baked a cracked-wheat loaf and planted lavender beside chimney. I wrote for three hours in afternoon.

Doe and at least one of the fawns paid us a 7 p.m. visit and a family of raccoons moved down river along bank after dark. But the big news of the day was that the baby swallows left the nest this morning and tried flying, with greater and lesser success! One crouched on porch beam near nest while a parent flew in and fed him. Others flew about at low altitude. One flew back and perched for a time beside sibling, as if to give him courage. Big day on the front porch—but it seems late for a swallow family to be still here. Most have left for Brazil or Argentina by now.

A cock pheasant visited the feeder mid-afternoon and walked calmly away through front yard, cock-of-the-walk.

Flush of small birds—warblers? juncos? in trees and along river bank. Distinguished by bright yellow rump, only visible in flight. Obvious migrates, cannot yet identify.

River rising from its historic low.

September 20, 1988—It rained overnight and the day was overcast, cold and wet. River rising further.

The swallows are flying, longer and stronger, but still returning to the nest to be fed. They spend some time on porch, looking at the world from a new angle.

We have a small brown squirrel, saw him again today, and baby rabbit, both in side yard.

A cock pheasant flew, cackling, from behind woodshed as I went out for wood at 6:30 p.[m.] About an hour later, the doe and two fawns visited creek feeder, the doe pausing now and then to chase away another deer who was, it seemed, trying to join them.

Was able to make a bouquet of yarrow, and dandelions and other delicate yellow flowers. May be the last of the season.

In early morning three grouse were at the river feeder.

September 21, 1988—Thick fog in the river valley this morning after starry night. Cock pheasant at creek feeder 9:30 a.m.—probably the same one who frightened me with his sudden flight last night.

P. planted daisies beside fence in front and delphiniums beside shed in back. I looked up from writing to see her carrying a 50–lb. bag of peat moss across yard. We need a wheelbarrow!

Swallows now flying strongly. Indistinguishable at a glance from their parents. We watched them wait in the nest for a midday meal, then fly one by one out into the world again.

Perhaps the most beautiful day of the nine we've had so far. The fog cleared and a cool sunny day followed. Watched grasshoppers struggling in the grass below front porch, many birds, migrating small ones, in the trees, all right with the world!

The doe and two fawns paid a visit, punctually, just before 7:15, to the creek feeder.

Half moon rising.

September 22, 1988—Autumnal equinox. Fall arrived at 1:29 p.m., unnoticed as I drove P. to airport. She must go to Reno for a couple of days.

A beautiful day, cool and sunny. Cock pheasant paid a visit, on time at 9:20 a.[m.] at creek feeder. I imagine doe and fawns were here at 7:15 p.[m.] too, because the creek feeder is empty tonight.

A porcupine lumbered down the driveway ahead of me in dark at 8:15 p.m. Heard owl and coyote as I unpacked groceries from car.

At 9:30 p.m., heard sound like a cat screaming–sneezing (we've heard it before, a sound of violent sudden conflict) outside back porch. Went out there to find porcupine in ball with quills up, near feeder. Wonder if a raccoon or bobcat is walking around nearby with porcupine quills in his nose?

September 23, 1988—(First full day of fall.) Last theory above probably wrong, because I heard the sound from riverside downstream most of the night and into the morning. Hard to describe—about like a triple-loud magpie scream.

Another pretty day, partly cloudy and warmer than we've had. The swallows are still here, but quiet now and purposeful. When they are at the nest, they perch on the lip confidently rather than huddling inside. They have matured quickly.

Pheasant paid regular mid-morning visit to creek feeder, this time with *three* hens! They ate the feeder dry and then circled slowly through grass to river feeder where they cleaned *it* up!

A whitetail deer visited re-filled creek feeder in mid-afternoon. And right on time, the doe and two fawns arrived at 7:20 p.m.! They stayed more than half an hour, walked across bridge and down-river.

On a day when I could have written at length, I puttered instead—glued broken mullion on bathroom window … mounted thermometer at kitchen window (I want a more elegant recording thermometer) … cleaned out shed a bit, fixed plug on bookcase lamp … pulled a few Kosha weeds … broke off on a fish, casting from bank after sundown. I visited schoolhouse, which is being insulated today … Called Bernie to find that Bud Benjamin died, memorial service Friday 30th. I will miss it. He was a very fine man and I feel a bit shaken by the news.

Now I must buckle down to a week of serious writing.

The last flowers on the place faded with the summer. I'd be hard-pressed to make a bouquet of what's blooming now. The petals of the last bouquet of summer are falling on the dining table.

River continues to rise as ranchers return irrigation water and drought relents.

Sept. 24, 1988—Cock pheasant on time, about 9 a.m., creek feeder. Spent most of the day in Bozeman, got back in time to leave three bright Jonathon apples for deer, who came to the creek feeder after dark. Skunk humped along river bank moving down river before sunset.

The willows on opposite bank of river becoming more vividly gold each day. River still rising. Must be nearly back to normal!

September 25, 1988—Sunday. Full moon. The nights are cool, 36° last night. Days in low 60s. Today a hard wind from the South dropped a few dead limbs into the yard— 'widow-makers', Delbrook calls them. P. slept til late morning, recovering from Reno trip, then mopped cabin floor, making it gleam invitingly and baked a braided poppy-seed loaf. The wind whipped her daisies at the fence but did no damage to them. We had our regulars on time, pheasant in the morning (he dashed away across driveway when I got too close to the window) and doe and fawns in the evening. I replenished wheat and corn at small feed store in Whitehall. Found swallows still here, often gone from nest now, but still returning in afternoon to be fed. Caught and landed two whitefish in desultory fishing from bank. Watched a hawk attack small birds near river feeder. Have a new hawk book to look him up in.

September 26, 1988—Hawks are hard to identify. I finally settled on a species; the book then described the range: '10 to 20 pairs in the lower Rio Grande Valley.'

Pheasant at creek feeder a little late today—mid-morning. Skunk and porcupine came across bridge late afternoon, doe and fawns on time before dark, lone deer who seems to shadow the doe & fawn family got to feeder later.

10° colder today, high of about 50°, and windy, from southeast, shifting to southwest.

Walked to schoolhouse. Colors from the height noticeably more autumnal. Found big rattlesnake skin shed outside a den up there.

Swallows are still here. I saw them flying high above the house in late afternoon, climbing much higher than I'm used to seeing them, almost out of sight. They are rarely at nest now.

P. hosed decks today. Cabin looks better than at any time since it was finished. We even found enough blooms about—showy daisy, dandelion, new blanket flower blossoms, and the delicate yellow one (named by Delbrook the other day) to make a fragile arrangement after all.

Many rises on river in morning before wind came up.

I was up couple hours last night with ache in jaw. I was able to admire full moon, the 'harvest moon' I think, as it seemed to float into and out of clouds.

Completed first draft of 'Russian Dentist' for book today.

September 27, 1988—'Unsettled' as they say in the Irish weather forecasts. A fierce wind blew from the north for $1/2$ hour at 1 p.m. After that, things calmed down. Cloudy and cool, high didn't get much past 50.

P. went to Cardwell to talk to Chris Wagner about landscaping schoolhouse with wildflowers and aspens next spring.

Pheasant at creek feeder. Raccoons have been turning over river feeder in the night.

I went with Delmar to discuss removal of beaver-felled trees in old river bed. Water encouragingly up there, and in our creek.

Dinner with Delbrook and Mary at Bannock House.

I got in about 3 hrs of writing—a start on an essay about the misadventures in the OTR buses.

Swallows were here in morning. They may have flown south on the north wind this afternoon.

September 28, 1988—Today I had a strong sense of time flying away, like the swallows. A beautiful sunny day. From the fence line on the schoolhouse hill, the ranch lay below in a hundred shades of autumn color, cattail, willows, grasses from green through bright yellow and orange to crimson.

We saw 2 minks (I am sure of it) near creek feeder, and later one swimming across river ... running more often than walking, nervously on the move.

A trout upstream above bridge swam from under the beaver dam as we watched. The creek returns!

Doe and one fawn followed the shadowing lone deer to the creek feeder at the usual time, about 7:15 p.m. Where is the other fawn?

I caught another whitefish from the bank in ten minutes break from writing in mid-afternoon.

September 29, 1988—Picnic up-river where creek enters from opposite shore—herewith dubbed Picnic creek. Caught a small rainbow there in tail of run, then 2 whitefish, then a 13-in. rainbow for another illegal dinner—truit au bleu!

Saw a snake swimming river, pretty whitetail doe bouncing away from us in woods, froglet on way back to cabin.

Hen pheasant at creek feeder this morning, doe and *both* fawns in evening, other deer earlier.

Warm day—perhaps 68° for a high. These are memorable fall days on the Big Hole. Yet *another* bouquet, thanks to new blanket flowers, yarrow and surviving mustard.

September 30, 1988—Concentrated on writing. Pheasants and deer called at creek feeder. Mink running—

swimming along opposite bank of river. The screaming sound on downstream river bank after dark. Bald eagle flew down-river in afternoon.

Animal and bird list these 3 weeks:

White-tailed deer	pheasants
mule deer	grouse
raccoons	killdeer
porcupine	swallows
mink	robins
muskrat	bald eagle
skunk	heron
rabbit	golden eagle
*squirrel**	hawks
rainbow trout	owl
whitefish	warblers
turtles	magpies
frogs	woodpeckers
snake (swimming)	Canada geese (on roadside
rattler (skin)	pond)
	mergansers
	other ducks

[*no turkeys—and no brown trout! Didn't fish creeks this year.]

October 1, 1988—A quite remarkable first of October! Warm cloudless day with a slight breeze. Walked up to schoolhouse once more to see drywall installation. It has the effect of making the room smaller. But it will be an elegant and inspiring place to work.

The memorable scene of the day was the cock pheasant persisting against doe and fawn opposition having a go at the creek feeder. A vigorous repetition of the scene the first morning. Three weeks ago early at river feeder. The deer kept chasing the pheasant away, but he finally prevailed and had the corn and wheat to himself!

Recorded sound of pheasant crowing in front woods mid-afternoon. P. says accurately that it sounds like nail being quickly removed from an old board.

Heard geese in distance down-river.

Also heard gunshots for first time this fall. It is Saturday. A hunter walked upriver on opposite shore before sunset. Cars and trucks moved slowly along road or stopped. We were both irritated by obvious willingness of strangers to shoot on private land, and both worried about the pheasants and deer we've seen every day and feel we know.

October 2, 1988—Another cloudless, perfect day. Usual visits from pheasants and deer. Cleaned out the shed. P. hosed off the swallow nests and cleaned porches impressively. I wrote memoir of being born and early love of travel for book, which goes slowly. Walked up to see drywall at schoolhouse. In midmorning, when I went to river bank to count my 3 rises, I counted 17 before I could blink. A quiet Sunday, except for the exuberant, loud singing of the songbirds in the trees most of the morning.

October 3—Last day of three exceptional weeks of perfect weather, fires at night, closeness and beauty. We even accomplished some planting and cleaning up and writing, in not too intense a way.

Chris Wagner came from Cardwell to see schoolhouse and plan a job of simple landscaping, which will involve topsoil, wildflowers, aspens, paths and water, perhaps a sprinkler system in ground. P. thinks he's probably good at it.

P. restored soil around what seem to be the two surviving clematis on bank upriver and marked them with rings of stone. We took down fishing gear and put it away upstairs, and I packed computer gear for travel after starting one more chapter.

A cock pheasant at creek feeder at 5:30 p.m.—and, behold! another one at river feeder! *Two* pheasants are an event. Deer came as usual. P. saw furry creature in front woods after dark, probably porcupine we think.

The day was sunny and a little cooler. The brilliant yellow leaves are beginning to fall.

Among the best things have been the poached trout with its unforgettable sauce; the arrangements of wildflowers always on the table; the new FM antenna which gave us music whenever we wanted; the deer and pheasant, and especially the deer and pheasant the two times when they were at feeders together; the sight of the autumn coming on, a bit brighter each day; the walks to the schoolhouse along deer trails; the re-discovery of the fishing at Picnic creek; the reading at night by the fire, the half-sleeping, half waking in the mornings with a new day ahead of us.

Fischer-Dieskau Is Ill: The baritone Dietrich Fischer-Dieskau has canceled his performances with the New York Philharmonic on Saturday and next Tuesday, saying he is suffering from the flu. He was to have sung Mahler's 'Songs of a Wayfarer.' Instead, the orchestra will present an all-Tchaikovsky program, including 'Romeo and Juliet,' Francesca da Rimini' and the Fourth Symphony, with Leonard Bernstein conducting. Mr. Fischer-Dieskau's recitals on Nov. 3 and 5 at Carnegie Hall are still scheduled.

Letter

Dear P.,

Our hero just doesn't know what trouble he causes when he does this. You know what this means: It means that a couple from Norway has come all the way to New York to hear him, has taken a nice room at the Plaza and the boat trip around Manhattan, and that on Saturday, not being able to read English, they are going to settle into their seats at Lincoln Center, happily awaiting the Meistersinger ... And then Bernstein gives the orchestra the downbeat ... And 'Romeo and Juliet' fills the hall. Afterwards, they will have a terrible fight in the Palm Court and go to bed angry!

Really, he ought to show up. This item brought tears to my eyes!

Love,
Charles

My infatuation with Dietrich Fischer-Dieskau led Charles and me on an hilarious quest spanning ten years and covering two continents before we leaned back, me sated and Charles victorious, on a plush banquette in New York City's Russian Tea Room. The craving to hear in concert one of the greatest voices of the twentieth century began innocuously enough one morning as I caught snatches of an early CBS arts show—kicked off the air by *Sunday Morning*—while going about my chores. I wasn't paying much attention to the television as I watered the pots of white petunias hanging in the dining room, picking off a spent bloom or a yellowing leaf as I went, conscious of, if anything, Able Baker Charlie Dog's growing impatience for his breakfast. Gradually, I became aware the house was being flooded with the most gorgeous sound I ever heard. I stopped in front of the television set, Able Baker's bowl in my hand, standing stockstill, mesmerized. Even filtered through muddy television amps, the sound could not be denied. It was breathtaking.

What I was hearing was a musical exploration of Mozart's *Don Giovanni* with the German baritone Dietrich Fischer-Dieskau in the title role. Fischer-Dieskau is not well known on this side of the Atlantic. One of the world's great singers, arguably the preeminent baritone of the century, he seldom appears here in the States. On those rare occasions when he does, he is unlikely to cross the Hudson River. I didn't know that then, assuming before long I would be listening to him in San Francisco's War Memorial Auditorium. To tide me over until I could hear Fischer-Dieskau in person I searched around and found a tape of the *Don* at a Berkeley music store. Charles dug up a LP of Schubert lied, the art song *Die Wintereise*, in New York. The chase was on.

Each fall I checked the year's concert listings in San Francisco on the outside chance he might get to where I was and in New York on the off chance I might get there. Fischer-Dieskau did cross the ocean a time or two. I was never around when he was. The years rushed by. Neither my hero nor I was getting any younger. The professional life of a singer is limited. I became fretful.

'I'll never see him,' I grouched.

To which Charles replied, 'Yes, you will.'

Over the next few months, Charles placed calls to Fischer-Dieskau's agent, managing by dribs and drabs to get a year's schedule of appearances, a church in Berlin, a concert hall in Amsterdam. Working through his own schedule, speeches and *Sunday Morning* and special appearances, fairs, jamborees and folk festivals, Charles came up with a reasonable facsimile of his own year. Then, he insisted I write my commitments down, a slightly embarrassing task: 6 a.m. Monday—pick up fish carcasses at Caruso's in Sausalito. We made a date. On July 2nd we would take our seats in the 4th row center of the orchestra section at Den Norske Opera in Oslo, Norway. Flying from New York, Charles would meet me in Ireland, we would leave Mother to the kind ministrations of the staff at Cashel House, and, away, to hear the *Meistersinger*.

Charles, our poky and sometimes distracted driver, fearing I would be unconscionably reckless, took the wheel on the drive to the airport. At the entrance to Shannon just as the four lanes narrow to two, there is a major intersection with a stoplight. Driving even more slowly and carefully than usual, Charles was half-way through the light when he spotted three children accompanied by a lively dog, crossing the green sward paralleling the pavement, heading right into the traffic. He slammed on the brakes. The driver of the car behind us, caught off-guard, slid into us with enough force to stow in the trunk of our tinny little car. All three of us were on the pavement in an instant, talking, motioning, apologizing, Charles insisting, it didn't matter, never mind, it's all right, we'll take care of it, don't worry, it's okay. We jumped back into our car, leaving the other driver to deal with his problem the best he could. We couldn't be worried about a bashed in rear-end. We had a plane to catch.

Oslo is a wonderful old city. Its central boulevard is crowned with an imposing hotel, resplendent in cut stone. Terraces tethered by blazing chains of geraniums hang like dowager gems around its glowing throat. A remnant of the past, the hotel's architecture is refined, understated, absolutely beautiful. Entering its doors was like walking into an Audrey Hepburn–Cary Grant movie. We made ourselves at home. I breakfasted on the terrace, swaddled in a thick white terry cloth robe, sheltered behind huge sunglasses. Charles, debonair as ever, handed me the city with a wave of his hand.

163

We left the hotel early that evening, giving ourselves plenty of time to stroll the avenue, pausing to glance over the notices of the Festival pasted in all the windows of all the newsstands and theaters. We couldn't read Norwegian. We didn't need to. We scanned the playbills until our eyes fell on the name Dietrich Fischer-Dieskau. Exchanging knowing little smiles, we resumed our promenade. Settling into our seats at Den Norske Opera house, we heard an announcement in Norwegian, held our breaths, stiffening when the engaging Lucia Popp walked out onto stage amid thoughtful applause and began singing. The *Meistersinger* had canceled.

Back at the hotel I railed at the fates, leaving Charles exasperated until the unfairness of my tirade recalled to him one, or maybe two, serious flaws in my character. I regret that argument as much as any we ever had. I seize this opportunity, Charles, for a public *mea culpa*.

'He's a singer, Mr. Kuralt,' his agent repeated each time Charles called for an assurance that Fischer-Dieskau would appear. 'He's a singer. Things happen. He gets a cold. He stays home. He's a singer.'

Eight months later in another part of the world, Charles rose from his seat, bowed slightly from the waist. 'Welcome to New York, Sir.' Our *Meistersinger* looked pleased. He stopped, smiled, shook hands. Charles motioned to me. 'She has come from San Francisco to hear you.'

It was at the Plaza's Oak Room where Kathleen, Charles and I were having lunch. Moments earlier, Charles leaned toward me, whispering, 'Look at the next table.' A straight-backed, silver-haired man with chiseled features was conversing with a smartly-dressed woman, who listened with rapt attention. It was Dietrich Fischer-Dieskau in town for a week's singing at Carnegie Hall.

The Friday evening performance of Fischer-Dieskau singing Mahler with the Philharmonia Orchestra of London caught us unawares, leaving us scrambling for tickets. Charles was triumphant when he announced a few days before the performance he had come up with three seats side by side in the balcony. I was overjoyed. Kathleen accepted the excitement, which she did not completely share, and the invitation to come along, agreeing to take a long week-end from work to hear my hero sing. By the time we three reached our seats at the top of the hall I was breathless with excitement. Kathleen was breathless with a rising terror. We left the glittering crowd behind us as we climbed to seats so far above the stage and tilted at such a dizzying angle, Kathleen clutched both Charles and her arm rest through the entire performance in an unexpected attack of vertigo.

I wept at Mahler's *Kindertotenlider* (on the death of children.) Though Charles admired the perfect control of the singing, at intermission he observed to Kathleen I never sobbed like that over any of his work. Even the adoration of the young couple sitting next to us overcome by the good fortune of hearing Dietrich Fischer-Dieskau in live perform-ance and sitting, for heaven's sake, next to Charles Kuralt— in the balcony of Carniege Hall, no less—could not totally make up for Charles' nagging sense of betrayal. Charles indulged me in any enthusiasm, raced to catch up, passed me by with his 'It's easy, you can do it' smile. A hint of personal attachment for anyone other than himself was met with a look of consternation. Charles' enthusiasms were intellectual. He expected mine to be the same.

Two more nights plus one afternoon wrapped in the elusive joy of the pure, perfect, human voice, now in art song recital with Hartmut Hoell on the piano, sealed my fate. I swore I would go anywhere to hear Fischer-Dieskau sing. I did go to a place or two, but I only heard him sing in concert one other time. It was in London though not before I sat more than once in audiences whose stifled groans rent the concert hall at the half expected but desperately hoped against announcement. We regret to inform you Dietrich Fischer-Dieskau will not be performing tonight.

Except for the first of the week's performances on Friday night, I left our room alone to walk the short block to the recitals at Carnegie Hall. Kathleen had flown back to her job on the West Coast, humming snatches of melody from Cabaret which Charles thought was a necessary antidote to Mahler (why, Charles demanded referring to the Nazi anthem in the musical, do the bad guys get the best songs?). Charles, incredibly, begged off further performances suggesting I give the extra ticket, now upgraded to a red plush box seat, to some struggling music student standing forlornly in the cold. It was the week of the NCAA play-offs. The North Carolina Tar Heels coached by Dean Smith were demolishing rivals in their run for the championship. Charles didn't, to his credit, fly off to wherever the team was playing, but I left him sitting in an easy chair in front of the television set, a Tar Heel born and a Tar Heel bred. Barely glancing up as he kissed me good-bye, Charles would laugh delightedly.

'You are never going to let me forget this. Every time you get mad at me, you'll say, and you watched basketball while Dietrich Fischer-Dieskau was singing just down the street.'

In his tribute to Charles at his death, NPR's Scott Simon spoke of Charles' fondness for jazz. Doctor Billy Taylor, a regular on *Sunday Morning*, and Loonis McGlohon's piano trio kept the passion alive, but Charles' musical tastes were eclectic. In music as in so much of his life Charles was willing to plunge into another's churning sea eager to see what all the cheering was about. Among the first records he gave me was a Rachmaninoff symphony, the original sound track from the film *Black Orpheus*, and Marian McPartland playing *Sweet and Lovely*.

Before we met, I had already stumbled onto the jazz trumpet of Ruby Braff's *How Long Has This Been Going On?* on a 1956 recording and Teri Thornton's debut album of 1960–61 with the relaxed *What's Your Story, Morning Glory?* The 99¢ bins of LPs haphazardly filled with discontinued pressings at Raley's on Reno's South Virginia Street yielded up these treasures along with recordings by folk singer Theodore Bickel, opera diva Victoria Los Angeles and Wagner's *Ride of the Valkyries*. I didn't dive like Charles into a musical pool surfacing with a sure knowledge of its terrain. I dipped into available offerings snatching up pearls in a casual, untutored way.

It was Edna Huntford, the art director at Tyson-Curtis Advertising, who gave me Mozart. Edna, who escaped Europe on one of the last boats to sail before France fell to the Nazis, couldn't abide Wagner. 'Music for slaves,' she would remark scornfully. When she could no longer bear walking up to the house with the *Ride of the Valkyries* blaring from the windows, she presented me with a recording of a Mozart flute concerto. Now, I can't imagine life without the turbulent redhead. Charles preferred Beethoven. He would choose Bernstein conducting the *Ninth Symphony* over any Mozart on our shelf. He stopped whatever he was doing to conduct a measure or two himself, and with broad, sweeping arm movements and a decisive nod of his head, when the music reached a crescendo, Schiller's *Ode to Joy*.

> Joy, thou shining spark of God,
> Daughter of Elysium!
> With fiery rapture, Goddess,
> We approach thy shrine.

Charles was a latecomer to opera. When he arrived he headed straight for the sopranos. Maria Callas, Benita Valente, Kathleen Battle, Eileen Farrel. On a CD insert he has Callas' 'Caro nome' boxed in black with an exclamation mark beside it. Opera came early into my life. We second graders at Reno's Mount Rose Grade School hopped and strutted around our classroom to the triumphal march from *Aida* or the toreador's entrance in *Carmen*, whistles blowing, tambourines shaking, drum sticks clattering. Our beautiful, statuesque Miss Smith cheered us on our boisterous way. There was a long hiatus after those rousing marches which didn't end until I was a senior in high school, but Miss Smith had done her job well. When tenor Mario Lanza hit the movie screens, the record companies rushed to take advantage of a blip in opera sales, most notably by re-

releasing the masterpieces of Enrico Caruso. It was 1950. We were in Shoshone, Idaho, a dusty two blocks on either side of the railroad tracks leading to Sun Valley. The corner drugstore devoted a narrow space in the mezzanine to the old 75 rpms and the just out 45s. It was customary to play a record before you bought to see if you really wanted it or not. A phonograph was available for potential customers. I took full advantage of it, not buying many records, but playing every Caruso in stock.

Years later, sometime in the Eighties, when another Italian tenor, Luciano Pavarotti, thrilled the opera public with his soaring high 'Cs', Charles held a private competition between Pavarotti and the legendary Caruso. Venue: a Lake Tahoe townhouse. Time: Christmas. Seats: none (too exciting to sit still.) Medium: an old Magnavox phonograph. Program: a re-release of Caruso's 1904 *Immortal Performances* pitted against a 1980 release of Pavarotti's *Greatest Hits. Di quella pira. Cielo e mar! Vesti la guibba.* Charles stopping and replaying, arguing, laughing. We agreed the difference in technique was apparent even to novices like ourselves; Caruso so easy, as if anyone could replicate his genius; Pavarotti, magnificent, yet you knew no one else could sing like that. It was that difference that put Charles' vote in Caruso's column. I was torn. I didn't want to vote at all. I remembered hearing Pavarotti asked on television of the time he was booed during a performance at Milan's La Scala opera house. Pavarotti looked straight into the camera, 'They don't boo you if you are singing well.' I couldn't vote against a man like that.

For all Charles' wide ranging musical tastes—he enjoyed blues and bluegrass, Mercer, Mable and Johnny, the Tin Pan

Alley of Cohen and Cole Porter, gospel and Glenn Gould—rock 'n roll never crossed his radar screen. He was called to task once when he anchored a television special at the death of Elvis Presley. Charles' conclusion? The King was overrated. He was in agreement with Aaron Copland's assessment of the Beattles, clever but not great. The Grateful Dead, the Rolling Stones, Santana, sex and drugs and rock 'n roll, all were an indulgence for the kids to outgrow.

Charles tried his hand at a musical production once when he and Loonis McGlohon teamed up to write *North Carolina Is My Home*. Mr. McGlohon composed the music. Charles wrote the lyrics. He got a great kick out of working with the musicians, admired each and every one, was knocked out by their talent. The cast including Charles presented the production live several times, once flying to London, to modest acclaim. Something seems to have happened between conception and completion. For all its downhome appeal—*Dinner on the Grounds* and *Barbecue Blues* were sassy, evocative tunes when Charles sang them at home—the production has a tinge of the Chamber of Commerce about it. *North Carolina Is My Home* which began as a celebration ended as a promotion.

Around the same time, 1987, Charles hosted the first Charleston, North Carolina, Jazz Festival. He and blues singer Tom Winslow teamed up to write *Tobacco Warehouse Blues* for the opening. The moody chords of Winslow's music, the pathos in Charles' lyrics is missing from *North Carolina Is My Home*. The difference is astonishing. Even without the rending blues sound of Winslow's guitar and his fine singing, you know this time around, the two got it right.

Tobacco Warehouse Blues
(Lyric by Charles)

I got a black iron pot, pot don't have no meat,
Got an old iron cot, but that cot don't have no sheet,
Got a fine hound dog, but he won't come when I call,
Got a pieced-back shirt, and I ain't got no shoes at all.

(*Refrain*)

I got the 12¢ a pound tobacco warehouse blues.
All my work don't buy no meat or sheet or shoes.
If you're there, O Lord, tell me how I'll ever lose
These 12¢ a pound tobacco warehouse blues.

When that sun come up, I was out there with my crop,
I was hoeing them rows till the sun begun to drop.
Eat some beans and bread and lay down in my skin,
Wait for that hot sun to come back up again.

Well the crop come up, and I strung 'em up with twine,
Cure them leaves just as gold as apple wine.
I said, Sal, look here, at the crop I made this year
I said, market day, I'm goin' buy you a rockin' chair.

(*Refrain*)

Well, I climbed up there and I took my tobacco down,
And, I hitched that mule and drove my crop to town.
20¢ a pound or maybe 35,
That'd be enough to keep Sally and me alive.

Well, I stacked my crop on the warehouse floor real neat,
Thinking about the shoes I would buy for my bare feet.
Then, all at once the tobacco man came around,
And the auctioneer, he said 'SOLD!', 12¢ a pound.

(*Refrain*)

Well, they paid me cash, and I walked out in the air.
I said, Sal, you ain't' gonna get no rockin' chair.
At 12¢ a pound Mr. Bell don't sell no shoes.
Goin' home with nothin' but the tobacco warehouse blues.

Every penny I got I done already spent.
I owe the man for my seed and feed and rent.
Well, there's nothing to do but go lay down on my cot,
And think of all those things I still ain't got.

(*Refrain*)

'Life is not simple,' Charles would sigh.

'But ... ,' I would moan.

We tried to make it simple.

We locked the gates when we were at the cabin. A man up the road tells of seeing the Jeep parked in the clearing one afternoon. Believing this might be his only chance to meet Charles Kuralt, he climbed the gate walking the quarter mile through the marsh. He says the two of them had a nice conversation.

Another man, fishing the opposite bank noticed the cabin door open. He waded the river in hopes of meeting Charles. After we introduced ourselves—Hi. I'm Pat Shannon. So happy to meet you.—he spent long, painful minutes telling me of the imagined comings and goings on the Big Hole of the elusive Mr. and Mrs. Kuralt.

We stayed off the beaten path. At Derrynavglaun we felt anonymous until Ray Brady, the *Sunday Morning* business correspondent, began telling Charles amusing stories of vacations spent at a Conamara hotel where we stopped on occasion for tea.

We ignored fame. Not the schoolhouse nor the cabin nor Derrynavglaun has—or has ever had—a television set.

We pretended that the handful of people we visited were interested in both of us—a difficult fiction to maintain. Boo

Lichtenberg confided that for years she barely noticed I was in the room, so completely had she fallen under Charles' spell.

We tried to minimize the slings and arrows.

Interviewer: Are you married, Charles?

Charles: Yes.

Prolonged silence.

Interviewer: Well, Charles, how do you like the City by the Bay?

Charles: You know the first time I was in San Francisco…

I grew increasingly testy. At airports, where I once stood demurely to one side exhibiting my best Nancy Reagan smile, I now turned my back and walked away.

Charles! Charles Kuralt! I love your stories. I was just telling my wife …

Thanks, with a chuckle and a nod, wondering where the hell I had gone.

Charles held brooding to be our nemesis and wanted to banish it from our lives. If that was impossible, he would settle for excluding it from the daytime hours. Anxiety, angst, agonizing were best confined to those dark hours before dawn when sleep slunk away in a pesky funk. Charles would toss and turn awhile, tiptoe into the bathroom, draw a glass of water, pausing to look out the window, scanning the sky for Greek gods before gulping down a couple of sleeping pills. Coming back to bed, he would smoke a cigarette, silent, his forehead creased, his arm lying motionless on the covers, waiting for drowsiness to overtake him.

I languished day or night, morose whenever time stretched out empty without him. With the closing of San Francisco

Stocks, there was plenty of empty time. Charles suggested I become a gardener. He knew I harbored a longing for an English country garden at Derrynavglaun, filled with enchanted rooms, sweetly scented and deeply bowered. At the cabin we began to think of a boardwalk wending its way through the briars bordering the creek, coursing into a rope bridge tethered to the schoolhouse bluff. As it was we walked around the marsh, following the deer trail up the broad side of the tail end of the bluff and back through the scrub to get to the library. While breaching the creek would cut the distance by more than half, it was the romance of a hanging bridge that charmed us. Charles envisioned a rough running path for me, serpentine through the beautiful upstream meadow with a bench here and there for sitting and soaking up the sun. The log seats, Charles reasoned, would come in handy later on when we were too old to hunker down on the rocks at the picnic pool for our sandwiches of processed cheese slathered with mayonnaise.

I enrolled in the Inchbald School of Design in London determined to master the art of landscaping. I learned two things almost immediately. The first was I had been dreaming, all unknowingly, of Gertrude Jekyll herbaceous borders for Derrynavglaun. The second was our Montana meadow was crying out for the elegantly curved seat designed around 1900 by Sir Edwin Lutyens. Charles nodded approvingly at my description of beds filled with old roses and lavender but nixed the Lutyens bench. Too formal for Montana.

The family gathered at the cabin for Christmas, Charles, me, Mother, Kathleen, J.R., Shannon and Shannon's dreamy-eyed boyfriend, Robley. My winter break assignment from Inchbald was to design a park. A howling wind sent the temperature plunging to well below zero. Undeterred, we stretched measuring tapes and imaginations, estimating the length of careless paths weaving through the underbrush and the spans of cable needed to traverse the creek. Back at school I drew plan after plan for Charles to scrutinize during his trips to London.

Inchbald was a honeyed sip of Zelda Fitzgerald's phantasmagoric elixir. On the brink of middle age, Zelda, made dizzy by the ceaseless tattoo of notoriety pulsing around her famous husband, Scott Fitzgerald, cleared a floor in a Southern mansion, installed barres and mirrors, stood, exposed in her satin slippers, feet *ouverte*, arms *en avant*, as the world watched. Too much competition, too many people, too much celebrity, too many seductions. The dance too frantic. The music too loud. Madness set in.

When Charles fixed me with a frantic look, while driving to Gallatin Field to catch a 6 a.m. flight to New York, repeating in that desperate tone, 'Well, we've got to do it, don't we?', my heart pounded. But in the end, we couldn't do it. He couldn't leave. I couldn't stay.

Over the years, Charles said to me whenever an acquaintance pushed too hard, 'We are not going to be captives of those rich folks.'

But, we were captives of someone, still in all.

At the end of Inchbald's spring break I parked the jeep in the garage at Gallatin Field, bound not for London but for Derrynavglaun.

CABIN DIARY, 1989

September 1, 1989

Arrived yesterday. A deer snorted in front yard beside bedroom window, startling me at bedtime.

Rose, saw pair of turkeys beside front porch. Called P. in Ireland to tell her. She not coming, so nothing that follows matters much. // I walked and walked after this news, came back to house and played Mozart Requiem, which far too triumphant. Great emptiness, a physical feeling, and crippling guilt.

But—as to nature report: Turkeys returned at 5 p.m., circled house from front to riverside to back to creekside to big field, eight of them!

Swallow nest on front porch again. I can hear young ones but haven't sat out there to look as we did last Sept.

Infrequent rises on river. No sign of pheasant yet. A heron flapped slowly down creek at 8 p.m.

Fair day, high about 70. Low last night about 42, I'd say.

Ken Ryder called. Schoolhouse stairs and floor apparently finished. I haven't been up there to see. I was waiting til Monday to see with P. for first time together.

I was going to make a big beef stew and gather flowers on the weekend.

Bob Schakne died of cancer.

September 2, 1989—Turkeys came to upstream fence in morning. A fierce NW wind rose at 3 p.m. and has blown all afternoon. Blowing hard at 10:30 p.m.

Yard overgrown in tall grass. Gaillardia (blanket flowers) here and there.

September 3, 1989—I thought of Roberta today, who saw no animals. Turkeys at 8 a.m. and again after 5 p.m., describing the same circuit, front to back of house. They didn't fly even when I came out on back steps to photograph them, merely continued their ambling and feeding, counter-clockwise around house. Deer, alone, along creek at 5 or so. Raccoon family at creek feeder at 8 p.m., little ones eager and skittish, like the young turkeys; dominant turkeys and raccoons, (like ducks and chickens) chase others away from food.

Went up to the schoolhouse. It is—magnificent! But what the hell to do with it now? I brought a rug for the front corner from China. Silk. I'm going to take it up there tomorrow and leave it, a sacrifice to the old building.

A fine, cloudless, cold day, calm, fish rising. I cast from bank and caught a hapless whitefish to break up writing, which I worked at hard from 1 p.m. to 8 p.m.

Very lonely at night. I have a frozen dinner (Swanson beef pot pie best so far) and do a crossword puzzle and listen to 105.5 which now Dvorak, Chamber Music Society of Lincoln Center, Piano Quintet in A Major. Coyote in hills to west.

Labor Day—Sept. 4, 1989—This was the day P. was to arrive. It was a perfect day, cloudless, cool in morning and evening. Turkeys at 7:30 a.m. and 5:15 p.m. They are almost used to my stepping out back door to photograph them.

No pheasants yet, and deer come only after dark. I walked out to the bridge at sunset and sent three white tails scurrying for the woods on the other side of the creek.

Heron flying low upriver at noon, fish rising. Caught a small brown from rip-rapped bank in 5 min and went back to computer. A terrible day to be indoors.

Swallow nest empty after all.

Sept. 5, 1989—Mystery of the ghastly screams at night solved at last! They are raccoons quarreling. Tonight, I shined the flashlight on four young ones, tan and—'cute' is the only word—fending off two others, apparently from another family, from a meal of corn I'd left for the turkeys west of house.

I overslept the turkeys this morning. At 8, they were already beyond the fence upstream, having scratched and eaten most of the corn at the shed.

The mild, beautiful days were ended by a hard raw wind from the west at 1 p.m., clouds rolled in, temperature dropped, but no rain yet.

Young deer at feeder at creek at 7:30 p.m. when I stopped writing to go feed the animals. He saw me and walked away briskly over the bridge and up the creek. Turkeys came in force again about 6, 10 at least, including young ones. I've shot 3 rolls!

Kathleen, Mama and J.R. all called today to be friendly. Had a good long talk with J.R. just now.

Wonderful Mahler Symphony #4 on KRIC.

'Posted' fence posts to keep out bird hunters with my new fluorescent-orange spray can.

Delbrook threatens a visit tomorrow, allegedly to offer the ranch for sale.

Writing: OK quality, low quantity.

No fires, no flowers.

September 6, 1989—Overcast and breezy and raw, but no rain.

The best thing happened a few minutes ago at 7:30 p.m.—two spotted fawns came to feed in the weeds and wildflowers just outside the living room window. And a few minutes later, with Haydn's 101st Symphony playing on 105.5—Solti and the Chicago Symphony—another young deer appeared in front, very nervous, lifting her head each time the music became louder, and once pausing with a front leg curled in the air to listen to a fast violin passage— whitetail listening to Haydn!

The turkeys came only as far as the front fence in the afternoon.

I wrote all day, pausing to make the beef stew I'd planned for P's arrival, so as not to waste all the ingredients. So I have an immense bowl of stew in the refrigerator tonight, and a bit heating on the stove—the first real meal of the month …

Hear, but did not see, a pheasant in the back. Ventured out of doors only a few minutes today, but still finished only 5 pages.

September 7, 1989—It was like a Disney movie around here today between 7 and 8 a.m.—a family of turkeys in front, family of *grouse* [see Sept 10] at creek feeder, and a family of deer passing through the side yard going south— the two spotted fawns and parents!

Raccoon family visits every night

No swallows—they must have left early this year. And I have not yet seen a pheasant! [See Sept. 10—yes you have.]

Called Wanda for her birthday. She sounds fine. Called Chris Wagner. He busy but will visit.

September 8, 1989—Cold, overcast most of the day, and windy. Never got above 50°. The turkeys called late— about 9—and early—about 4:30—all ten of them. Grouse at creek feeder, and later young raccoons.

Delbrook visited, looking strained. He wants to sell the ranch for $1^1/2$ million dollars. Why, for only about $2^1/4$ million we could own the whole valley! (The other ranch hasn't sold yet.) He says he has until 1993 to give Boo her share. His price is for 1050 acres plus BLM land—about half again as much as they are asking downstream.

What with one thing and another including shortage of inspiration, only got 3 pages written in spite of long hours at the machine. Must greatly increase output in next 10 days.

Washed socks and underwear, my first go-round with the washer and dryer! Worked out okay.

September 9—We moved the desk into the schoolhouse. Everybody felt celebratory. I felt like crying.

It dominates the room.

Jerry and Ken spending the weekend on window details. I invited them down to dinner and fed them the beef stew and three bottles of red wine. I deeply cut my finger—damn near sliced the top right off– cutting apart a frozen bagel. Blood all over the kitchen and floor. We managed to stop the bleeding with many layers of Kleenex and tape. They stayed until 1:30. To bed feeling hurt and stupid.

September 10, 1989—Turkeys spent most of the day outside the upstream fence, came into yard at 4:30 for an hour. This was my day to frighten away visitors … 5 grouse [pheasants] across creek flew when I went out there to leave them their corn … two deer trotted away from back porch when I went out after sundown for a few minutes of fishing from bank. A small fish rising just off rip–rap made a monkey of me.

Kathleen (at 8:30) Wanda, JR and even Shannon! called to say happy birthday. Wanda told me Kathleen still in trouble and seeing Yvonne again. I keep my fingers crossed for her.

My mother not much improved, my father says. Susan being forced out of job, Lisa says.

Clear, cold and windy, not much over 45° today.

Cut finger makes typing frustrating. I ache with loneliness tonight. I am 55.

I, too, was 55 and aching with loneliness.

Everyone was clamoring for Charles' attention. Steve Allen. Phyllis Schlaffly. Hunter Thompson. Gloria Steinem. CBS News. G.P. Putnam's Sons publishers. The University of North Carolina. The Governor of Montana. I was clamoring for Charles' attention. There wasn't enough attention to go around.

At Derrynavglaun I didn't need attention. The garden needed attention. With gritted teeth and manic energy I threw myself into the work at hand. A demented Charles, I would turn this sheep heaven into an English country garden worthy of Miss Jekyll herself. Anybody who didn't believe it, could just watch me.

The meaning of Derrynavglaun, *Doire na bhFlann* in Irish, is a source of contention with the locals. A resident scholar, Tim Robinson, has mapped and indexed Conamara, a task of enormous complexity in this largely ignored region. Mr. Robinson translates *Doire na bhFlann* as the 'wood of the Flanns,' a family he believes once lived here. None of my neighbors ever heard of a family named Flann. Mr. Robinson says by way of explanation it might be the first name of the man of the family rather than the surname. My neighbors insist Derrynavglaun means 'oak glen of the flowers.' On occasion I have relayed Mr. Robinson's defense of his interpretation to Mary and Sean King whose family owned the land for half a century. They carefully consider the facts; softly comes the reply.

'Tim Robinson. He's English, isn't he?'

That settles it. It is my oak glen of the flowers now. Russell Page, a garden designer of gargantuan proportions, spent a lifetime creating gardens for others, never to have one for his own. 'But, I allow myself daydreams,' he wrote in his eloquent *The Education of a Gardener*. 'I would rather start with an old garden, however badly arranged and however neglected, since a few mature trees, an old wall and even a few square yards of good soil will give me the advantage of a twenty year start, all the more so as I shall be so late a starter.' Mr. Page gave me courage.

Before Derrynavglaun was mine it belonged to three bachelor brothers, Tommie, Marty and Joe Mannion. One brother was the farmer, one a fisherman on the Ballynahinch waters which this piece of ground borders, and one was a blacksmith. Eileen Hines, who lived on the hill behind me before age and infirmity took her off to an old folks home, told me stories about the brothers.

The outlines of long, narrow mounds which can still be seen on the hillsides were lazy beds. The Mannions grew potatoes in these strips. Year after year the sheltered, sunny slopes produced the first potatoes in the valley, a source of great pride to the brothers. They shared the bounty, carrying huge bags of freshly dug spuds to families whose supplies from the year before were dwindling. If a neighbor's cow was dry, they would come unannounced before dawn to stash a can of fresh milk in the turf pile where it was sure to be found when it was time for the morning fire to be lit. Children sneaked into the orchard under the very noses of the brothers. They stole crisp apples from the gnarled, lichen-covered apple tree escaping scot-free. The brothers always brought flowers, bunches of hydrangeas, pale blue as the ocean whipped with foam; cala lilies on long stocks; thorny-stemmed red roses impervious to all those blights under which modern roses swoon and die.

The Mannions carved out a farm on this hilly land fixed between the watery bog and the barren Bens, an abrupt chain of mountains looming behind Derrynavglaun. Those old men had a sophisticated understanding of land use which provided the blueprint for a graceful transition from sheep farm to ornamental garden. I discovered early on I wouldn't go wrong if I paid attention to the brothers. Designers spend lifetimes trying to create what those three Irishmen left behind for me to play with.

It was hard to make sense of at first. The patterns were only partial, the lines indistinct. Windbreaks of out-of-control trees and bushes stretched out awkward limbs from deformed trunks made grotesque by generations of nibbling sheep. Cursorily piled rocks filled gaps in the stone walls dividing the land into ever smaller plots. The close cluster of cottages and sheds just about filled the only level course of ground. In the process of clearing away a decade or two of debris and overgrowth, I gradually became conscious of the essential logic of the Mannion farm.

Derrynavglaun is an irregular rectangle running north and south. The northern end flares out into a mushroom shape at the top of a small hill, its form determined by the contours of the hilly terrain. A long slope of land sweeps down and away from the narrow flat concourse. By the time it has leveled out below, it is bogland. The Mannions divided the farm into an informal series of what landscapers elegantly call garden rooms. Some of the Mannion rooms were meant to be flower and vegetable patches; most were used for the practical affairs of farming: hay field, manure pile, separate quarters for the ewes and the rams. Not having any ewes or rams except for the occasional uninvited transient, I conflated several of the rooms, reducing the total number to five: entryway, courtyard, orchard, kitchen garden, green sward.

While I learned more reading Russell Page's *The Education of a Gardener* than I did from my rollicking days as a student at London's Inchbald School of Design, neither the book nor the school came close to preparing me for the trials of gardening in Conamara. The actual backbreaking work of clearing and cleaning was the least of it.

There is one immediate discrepancy between the books a would-be traveler browses through and the reality of the Emerald Isle. It is the weather. The illusion of endless soft, misty days punctuated by brilliant sunshine is shattered when one learns it takes 48.75 inches of rain spread out over 250 days of the year to form the bogs for which Ireland is so justly famous. That means rain two days out of every three. Weather forecasts predict either intermittent sun or intermittent rain. Yearly sunshine is totted up in hours not days. The tempestuous Atlantic ocean seizes this small northern island in its embrace and subjects it to all of its many moods.

A woman of my acquaintance once summed it up for me, 'Ah, the rain; we would be lonely without it.'

A second rarely discussed feature of the Conamara land-scape is the midge. Peculiar to Ireland and Scotland, the midge is nature's equivalent of the United States Air Force's Stealth bomber. This scourge of the rural West hibernates on the rare, wonderful days when the sun shines and the wind blows and heaven is at home among the lakes and the bogs. But on moist, warm, close, cloudy days, watch out! Microscopic cousins of the Montana mosquito hatch by the zillions. Billowing clouds erupt out of the soil zeroing in on fleshy targets with relentless ferocity. Banding together, they form dense, whirling patterns clearly visible to the youngest child. 'Oh, midgets,' little girls shriek, stampeding to the nearest doorway.

My first encounter with midges came while digging in the Mannion's old rose hedge. It was a fine June evening. Warm, misty, still. Like the pictures in those travel books. Bareheaded, bare-legged, bare-armed, I went as the unsus-pecting Gael into battle against unimagined odds. One or two innocent thrusts of the trowel into the deeply manured bed disturbed the ancient slumber of hoards of midges. Surrounded and attacked, in less than a minute not an inch of exposed skin remained unbitten. I flapped my arms, shaking my head wildly in a frenzied caricature of a pagan dance as I was driven, dazed, from the garden.

Midges are particularly savage in the late hours of the day, the sacred, still moments of dusk. It is my personal opinion that the cocktail hour grew out of man's desperate attempt to escape the wrath of the bog gods by slipping into a shadowy apse at sunset, there to sip the hallucinatory inoculant pouring, chilled and refreshing, from the lip of a golden goblet.

There is a third and final bane Derrynavglaun gardeners must brave. This affliction is the hardest to bear because its elimination, so simple in concept, is so elusive in practice. I spent much of my young life in sheep country, north-eastern California, northern Nevada, southern Idaho. On summer vacations I lounged around Basque sheep camps drinking spring water, eating freshly-baked bread, watching American sheep grazing slowly, methodically, without fuss or undue effort. I never in all those summers saw one jump.

The sheep of my childhood are barely recognizable in the breed raised around Derrynavglaun. The Conamara sheep is no pastoral animal. It has long, unkempt hair and bulging eyes. Indecipherable graffiti in ubiquitous reds and blues decorate its back as if it had been attacked by some lunatic abstract artist. The Conamara sheep is a wily, sly, treacherous creature knowing no fear and committing acts of incredible daring to get what it wants. What it generally wants is a flowering plant. Roses are what these sheep covet; they will settle for clematis. In a pinch they will daintily dine on any berry or leaf labeled ornamental.

One lackluster morning, following a convivial Irish evening, I was gazing dull-eyed and empty-headed out J.R.'s arched windows over the bog to the slopes of Cashel Mountain when a movement somewhere to the far right caught my attention. As I tried to adjust my focus, a sinister suspicion crept into my mind. I walked, squinting, to the door. After several years of invasion, the fences around our two acres had finally been made secure against marauding livestock. Barbed wire, rock, concrete ringed Derrynavglaun. So, how could it be? How could a sheep be grazing not far from my David Austen 'Heritage' rose bushes, munching her way steadily and deliberately toward them? Not waiting for an answer to surface, I raced across the meadow, my nightgown billowing around me, arcing below the cursed animal. As I said, Conamara sheep are smart. When they see a wild woman approaching, they head for a known escape route. If you follow a sheep who is trying to get out of a place, she will lead you directly to the weakness in your fortifications which allowed her to get in in the first place. I pursued the rogue ewe, evading the septic tank, open ditches and clutches of briars, but I wasn't good enough. By the time I reached the orchard toward which she ran, the ewe was placidly grazing outside the garden, several yards down the road.

I bolted through the gate to the parking lot, pacing back and forth along the orchard wall judging heights, scrutinizing the grass for hoof prints, straining to see a few strands of wool caught on a rough surface, seeking a small rise or a boulder which might have elevated the ewe enough to volley her over the four foot embankment. I couldn't find anything. I retreated into the house assuming a combat-ready stance. Within fifteen minutes, the ewe was back in the garden. All that day the ewe and I battled, me hunkered helpless before her guerrilla tactics of hit and run. Time after time, my first glimpse of her would be at the moment she, with a gentle tug, would pluck a leaf from this or that prized plant. She would see me coming, head for the orchard and make her escape before I was close enough to determine the exact spot of her exit. By nightfall I was exhausted.

I set the alarm for half five so I would be ready for her first incursion the next morning. It was barely light. She was already in the garden grazing contentedly along the rock wall. A second day of stalking and failure left me exasperated and hopeless. I drove over to the King's, whose sheep graze in the fields surrounding Derrynavglaun, to put my case to them. Mr. King agreed to come the next day and take the outlaw to the mart at Oughterard, getting rid of her once and for all. The only question he had was, which ewe was it. I told him not to worry, I knew which ewe it was.

Just to be sure I knew, I was positioned on the wooden bench on the front terrace the following morning when the first rays of dawn struggled through an overcast sky. I sat looking intently at the stone wall. Then, I saw her. She came over the wall with all the ease of a whitetailed deer. It wasn't through the orchard she came. She sailed over the wall below the gatehouse. Well, that was impossible. The road runs smack against the stone in that area of the wall, no boulders, no rises to assist the jump, no straight approach where she might mount a running start. No one would believe me when I told them the ewe jumped the wall there.

She knew I saw her and trotted carelessly up through the orchard and down over the wall. Now that I knew where she jumped in, it was easy enough to make out the hoof prints at the base of the fence. When Mr. King arrived, I pointed out the evidence and described in detail the markings of this particular ewe. Mr. King was non-committal. He didn't take up my offer to walk the fields with him and point out the offender. He set off alone, stopping on the way back to tell me he would return to take her away. Toward evening I saw two men walk into the field and return with a ewe bound hand and foot. She was tossed without ceremony into the boot of the car.

I slept in a little the next day, rising and drawing open the drapes well after the sun rose, yawning, checking the weather. There she was. I was dumbfounded. I went yowling out the door. She watched me coming. Just before I reached her, she sauntered slowly toward the orchard.

Now I was mad. I had been deceived. I sat at my computer pounding out a notice:

Wanted

Man with trailer to capture renegade
ewe and transport her to Ballinafad.

Will pay £50

Telephone 3 46 45.

I printed out the proclamation and drove to the shop at Recess, where I handed it over to the obliging shopkeeper. It was not long before Mr. King was over to say he would take out the rogue ewe as soon as a friend, Sean Keaney, was free to help him. Mr. King wasn't warm and friendly. He pointed out they had taken one ewe the day before. Reluctant but resigned, Mr. King allowed me to walk the fields and finger the culprit. When I pointed her out Mr. King was disbelieving. The ewe was young, only a year old. Young ones couldn't jump that way, Mr. King said. They didn't have the strength for it. I held my ground. That night Mr. King and Sean Keaney came and got her. Mr. King knocked on my door inviting me to come out to the car. He insisted I look into the boot where the ewe lay perfectly still and uncomplaining. It was her all right. I felt a pang of guilt. Now she would go to the mart well before her time. Damned animal. Why wouldn't she behave herself?

Charles was indifferent to my complaints about the rain. He didn't believe me when I told him about the midges. About the sheep he was confident of the solution. Eliminate the problem, he said. Get rid of the sheep. Buy them. Find them a new home. Mr. King will be happy. You will be happy. I will be happy. As it turned out Charles' solution didn't make Mr. King happy, but the problem gradually took care of itself. The miraculous ewe, the best of her breed, had been eliminated. Others tried to take her place and failed.

I became calm, if not altogether happy, working steadily with some degree of success.

These days the rough semi-circle of the entryway is filled in the spring with yellow roses, 'Graham Thomas', 'Alister Stella Gray', 'Windsong', banded by a swath of berberis blooms. A giant sycamore in the courtyard looms over the grape hyacinth volunteers which crowd into the formal beds vying for our attention with tall, white natives, kissing cousins of our Shasta daisy. The massive climber, 'Rambling Rector', covers the end of the terrace with sweetly-scented clusters of white roses even as a trio of lavender spikes try to cheer a disconsolate 'Gloire de Dijon' struggling against blackspot and mildew.

In a moment of bravado, a friend and I transported three thirty-foot oak trees from County Wicklow to add to the five survivors from the Mannion days. We did our best, staking and fertilizing, tending to them tenderly, but the rigors of Conamara proved too much for these immigrants from the east of Ireland. A few leaves waved a rueful farewell before the tall trunks succumbed to a final homesickness.

The kitchen garden remembering, perhaps, its glory days under the Mannion's care, sprang to life with the help of a truckload of kelp. Such a quantity of vegetables, beets, rhubarb, green onions, strawberries, and of such an enormous size, blanketed the plot, I may be forgiven for thinking I beat the odds and came up a winner.

Derrynavglaun is not the English country garden I envisioned, but it is not quite an Irish garden, either. It is a garden Russell Page would understand, more present in the dream than in the reality.

Clipping, *New York Times*, March 24, 1990

> March 24, 1990 NYT Donal Henahan: 'The Metropolitan Opera's new 'Don Giovanni,' its first staging of Mozart's Olympian tragicomedy … Samuel Ramey, the handsomest … Don Giovanni on the stage today … '

Letter with two unused tickets

Dear Pat,

For Henahan, this is a rave! We missed the premiere, but they've put it in the repertory for the rest of this year and all of next year, so we can see it any time!

I've talked with Kathleen … just a few minutes ago … and she says to tell you that she loves you more than ever. She actually seems to be enjoying herself, making friends, having a fine time. J.R., he says he's hit a blank wall, doesn't quite know where to go next with his film project; he got roughed up in class last weekend, I think, everybody telling him he didn't have a good grasp of the characters and all that. I told him (1) everybody hits blank walls and (2) maybe he knows better than they do and (3) that I'd come help him as soon as I get this wretched book behind me in the next month. Your mother sounded cheerful today, completely over her bad spell, and even triumphant because the retirement home is going to pay her doctor bills and knock something off the rent for the time she had to be out of her room. I sent her a bit of extra walking around money (or slot machine money) this month to help make her feel better.

Of Shannon, I have only J.R.'s word that she's thriving, but still aimless about what to do next. Robley left home for J.R.'s visit, he says, and he gets the feeling Shannon is impatient with Robley again and would like him to go away.

I spent the week making speeches mostly, but almost all those are behind me for a while now and I must concentrate on nothing but the book. I have about two-thirds of a book and grim determination, but not enough time to make it good and complete.

I am waiting for the line to clear to ask you about sheep and roses and rain …

Love,
Charles
March 25

The splendid isolation of gardening at Derrynavglaun was interrupted by a muted murmur, echoing faint over the bogland, a summons from the sirens of the swelling, surging sea. Charles was in New York. Kathleen in Nevada. Shannon in California. J.R. in Washington. I was alone with no one to bind me. I plunged, mad with excitement, into the frigid waters of the Atlantic Ocean.

I bought a boat. An open wooden sailing boat, a Galway Hooker. The *St. John* was fashioned on the shores of Mweenish Island in the Irish-speaking Gaeltacht by the legendary Clogherty family in 1907. Her birthplace a bay away from Derrynavglaun became for me the portal to a haven free of misgivings, devoid of celebrity, rooted in community and faith and tradition. I secreted all my lost hopes beneath the *St. John*'s sensual tumblehome and, all atingle, entered the doomed Padraig Pearse's 'little Gaelic kingdom.'

Charles attentive, rueful, non-committal, dispatched a log book and a copy of Moulton Farnham's *Sailing for Beginners*. Over the coming months, the post brought words of caution, descriptions of the latest safety gear, wind velocity charts and, almost as an after-thought, an allusion to the pleasure sailor's self-mocking summing up. A boat is a hole you pour your money into.

To the Irish in the West of Ireland at the turn of the twentieth century, that contemporary assessment would have been incomprehensible. The Galway Hooker was their lifeline. She linked remote islands to the commerce and culture of the mainland. Hookers carried cattle and horses from Galway, mail from America, turf from Conamara. The young playwright, John Synge, took Willie Yeats' advice to 'go to the Aran Islands. Live there as if you were one of the people themselves; express a life that has never found expression.' Synge left us eloquent writings and sepia-toned photographs chronicling a people entwined with the sea.

By 1960 the last working Hookers were on anchor or abandoned dockside. They weren't needed anymore. Ferries, power launches, airplanes, helicopters, safe and sure, did what the Hookers used to do and did it better. Some men couldn't say goodbye. The O'Briens and the McDonaghs and the Baileys kept their boats and kept them sailing. The *Capal*, the *Toni* and the *Maighdean Mhara* were eyed by doubting men who, one by one, lost their doubts and reclaimed rotting black hulls all along the Gaeltacht coast. Caulking, nailing, painting, the Darbys, the Macs, the Cualains and Cheonins and Caseys set off a Hooker revival.

A Galway Hooker has a black hull and blood red sails. It is fashioned of oak and larch, the hand-sawed timbers soaked in barrels of hot water and bent by hand to form her bold, broad belly. Giant tree trunks are chiseled into masts capable of withstanding the Atlantic's gales. There are no blueprints; measurements are the currency of the boat builder. Hookers are stamped with the signature of the maker. Irish-speaking boatmen, the *badoiri*, can tell at a glance which boats are Glogherty-built, which by a Casey, which by a MulKerrins.

Nor do the men who cut and stitch the sails use any pattern except the one in their heads. When Johnny Bailey and his sons cut the sails for the *St. John*, all they required was a ball of twine and a handful of nails to calibrate the measurements, a hall floor large enough to lay out the canvas, and a pair of sharp scissors. The whole process, including a drive along the coast and a pint of Guinness, took less than a day.

Even with the revival, there are not many Hookers left. Dick Scott, a marine historian, sees the future of the boats as tenuous at best. Altogether there are maybe twenty *bad mor*, literally big boats, and *leath bhad*, half boats, still afloat. They range from 29 foot to 44 foot. Smaller *gleoiteog* and even smaller *pucan* bring the entire fleet to fifty, though you'll get an argument on either side of that figure.

The *bádóiri* race the gaff-rigged Hookers in contentious summer regattas up and down the Gaeltacht coast. The Roundstone race proved my undoing. It was there, on a day blessed by the fairies, that I first saw the black boats tacking up the bay, booms sweeping the froth off the whitecaps, red sails taut and eager, and heard the unfamiliar sound of Irish ricocheting across Hooker bows.

Native Irish-speakers make up less than five percent of the population of Ireland. They may look the same as their Dublin cousins, but they are a breed apart. A stubborn independence is the life raft which keeps the Irish language afloat in a world drowning in corporate blandness. A crackling vitality marks the Irish-speakers. They are quick, bright, funny, unpredictable, and totally engaging. Switching back and forth between English and Irish with alarming rapidity, they are impossible to beat out. Count it a good day if you stay even.

After buying the *St. John* and bringing her back from exile on the east coast, I anchored her at Mace pier outside the Gaeltacht village of Carna. A dirt road, west of Carna, meanders around and about an inlet dotted with low, white houses before petering out at a stone jetty where four or five small fishing trawlers tie up. Long, narrow curraghs, the sturdy in-shore craft resembling a cross between a rowboat and a canoe, rest on banks of stubby grass and rocky outcroppings. There is always a fisherman or two at work around the pier to help if you're having trouble with a boat. You can get a cup of tea at any door you knock on. The tea, the chat and the easy introductions—'She's a Yank; she bought the *St. John*' by way of explanation—were a counterbalance to a wretchedness I was loath to admit.

Charles was still doing *Sunday Morning*, giving speeches, working on CBS specials. We met at the cabin or in Reno or at Tahoe or San Francisco for family reunions, but he never again came to Derrynavglaun. The late night knock on the door, the early morning telephone call, the tea and the chat were the last things Charles wanted. What I welcomed as a jubilee, Charles reckoned an invasion.

I wanted to write a book about the *St. John* and the people I came to think of as family. Charles counseled against it. He knew the pitfalls an inexperienced writer could stumble into while artlessly committing to paper what had before been only pub talk. As usual I did not listen. Hunching, droop-shouldered, determined, over the little PowerBook Charles gave me for what he considered a ill-fated project, I wrote and re-wrote and re-wrote the rewrites. Charles read chapter after chapter, editing, re-editing, caught between affection and exasperation. At one point he exploded, 'You have included everyone in Conamara.' 'I didn't want to leave anyone out,' I protested. I was so sure everyone in the Gaeltacht would be delighted with my adventure story. It was the thought of sitting in Moran's pub in Carna listening to the Irish-speakers arguing the truth of it that kept me at the keyboard. Finally, Charles had enough. He threw up his hands sending the whole mess off to Neil Nyren, his editor at G.P. Putnam's Sons.

Apparently, Mr. Nyren read it, as a favor to Charles, I suppose. He sent it back with the comment that it was a sweet book with absolutely no market. He proposed a condensation, a shorter version which could be offered to an anthology. No, contradicted Charles after thinking it over, it should be longer, a fuller view of life at Derrynavglaun. Once again, he repeated, it should be fiction. Not contented with two dissenting opinions, I sought a third. I sent a copy to my old friend, Bob Laxalt whose novel, *A Man in the Wheatfield*, is one of those books 'that no one knows,' and should. Bob contended the manuscript contained the germ of not one but two books. He proposed my spending a few months in his writing class at the University of Nevada as a start on getting it straightened out.

I thought, to heck with it. I'd rather be sailing anyway. I tossed the half dozen computer discs marked, seemingly at random, 'A Memoir,' 'A Yank in Conamara,' 'The Man Who Stayed Home,' drafts one, two, final, four, final, six, into a printed Christmas carton and concentrated on trying to beat the *Hunter* and the *Lord* at the MacDara's Day regatta.

When Mother lay dying in her small mother-in-law apartment at the rear of Roberta's Nevada home, I pulled out the discs, making another half-hearted stab at getting the manuscript finished. It was a nineties version of knitting. Charles and I met in Reno to be with Mother when a Scotsman, an ex-missionary, removed her gallstones. Charles' studied interest in a video of the operation remains a testament of his regard for her. The metallic instruments gliding over her dark, smoky insides lifted gallstones with more precision but less suspense than the small shovel retrieving a jawbreaker when a nickel is inserted in the candy machine slot. Mother who crossed the Southwestern plains in a covered wagon was more alive to the mystery than we were.

The month before the operation, I braved Mother's complaints to force feed her hand-ground turkey sausage and fat-free, milk ending the meal with slices of angel food cake topped with fresh fruit, once a favorite but now greeted with groans of, 'Oh, Pat, not again.' The doctors agreed she was healthy. Though she came through the operation just fine, it proved a turning point. Her energies declined and her will, so strong if so often impotent, failed. Roberta and I spent Mother's last month spelling one another, sleeping next to her, insisting she taste unwanted protein drinks, overseeing illusionary physical therapy routines, trying vainly to convince her to stay alive. A doctor friend of ours came to us with vitamin concoctions and convictions, lessening Mother's apprehension and our own sense of inadequacy. Michael

Gerber and his wife Inge have clasped our family's hands so tightly and on so many occasions, we are welded together.

Charles was not with us when Mother died. He was in New York announcing his retirement from CBS News. He reported from Lillehammer sending back stories from the XVII Olympiad. He returned to hand in the resignation he toyed with for so long. He called almost daily, sent cards, commiserated, but Charles did not come to Fallon. His absence at Mother's bedside warned of something terribly amiss. I was unforgiving of his cavalier treatment of the woman who loved him so, and I looked away. Not one to insist upon devotion as her due, it would have pleased Mother to see both her obituary and Charles's retirement printed on the same page in the Fallon weekly.

Charles' retirement was not a success. He held his own for almost sixty years. Ambitious, but not power hungry. Passionate, but moderate in judgment. Tolerant, but not without conviction. It was easy for him to walk away from a story. It was in his personal allegiances that he was conflicted. There were too many demands from too many people who claimed a piece of him. Much has been written of Charles' inability to say no, but ill and depressed he said yes to projects over which he had no control and which in better times he would never have considered. He said yes to a series of grueling television minutes written and researched by someone else which left him harried and distraught as he struggled with rewrites and tepid interviews. He said yes to a *New York Times* travel supplement lending his name for the first time in his career to an advertising venture …

He said yes to a television series from which, as his health failed, he was forced to withdraw, painful increment by painful increment. On the day before Charles died, a television producer sat by his bedside outlining his next assignment.

Charles and I met, uneasily, for a few days here and there during those last years. We made plans. We made promises. We prepared surprises. Charles gave me a 1908 edition of *The Collected Works of William Butler Yeats* printed by The Shakespeare Head Press. My gift to him, I decided, would be a 60-second update on Yeats's Ireland. This time, I would finish that troublesome book and make Charles proud of me. Weeks of furtive editing reduced a lumpy three hundred pages to a compressed memoir a third the original size, just enough copy for a quick take during an elevator ride, as CBS News colleague Andy Rooney once commented about a paperback of Charles's. An Irish friend handled the private printing as a surprise for Charles' sixty-third birthday. It was too late. The book came off the press a week after Charles died. The three hundred copies of *The Man Who Stayed Home* were a best seller at Kenny's in Galway town. I got my money back and a little spare change, but to my utter astonishment, Carna was outraged. As Charles anticipated, the men and women I admired found no comfort in being on the printed page.

It no longer mattered. The man who gave resonance to my life was gone.

Letter, Summer 1990

Dear Pat,

I chanced upon the Beaufort Scale on the ship to Alaska and copied it down for you, remembering that you asked once:

WIND FORCE	WIND SPEED IN KNOTS	DESCRIPTIVE	SEA CRITERIA	WAVE HEIGHT (FT.)
0	less than 1	calm	like a mirror	–
1	1 to 3	light air	ripple, no crests	4 inches
2	4 to 6	light breeze	small wavelets	6 inches
3	7 to 10	gentle breeze	large wavelets, crests begin to break.	1.5
4	11 to 16	moderate breeze	small waves, becoming longer	3
5	17 to 21	fresh breeze	moderate waves, many white horses, chance of spray	6
6	22 to 27	strong breeze	large waves begin to form, white foam crests extensive, spray	9
7	28 to 33	near gale	sea heaps up and white foam from breaking waves begins to be blown in streaks	12

WIND FORCE	WIND SPEED IN KNOTS	DESCRIPTIVE	SEA CRITERIA	WAVE HEIGHT (FT.)
8	34 to 40	gale	moderately high waves of greater length. foam is blown in well-marked streaks	16.5
9	41 to 47	strong gale	high waves, dense streaks of foam, crests of waves begin to topple	21
10	48 to 55	storm	very high waves with overhanging crests. foam in great patches is blown in dense white streaks. tumbling of seas is heavy	27
11	56 to 63	violent storm	exceptionally high waves, long white patches of foam, everywhere edges of wave crests are blown into froth, bad visibility	34.5
12	64 and over	hurricane	Air filled with foam and spray, sea white with driving spray, visibility very seriously affected	42 plus

I hate to even READ about anything over Force 6!

Love,

C.

We stood under the North Carolina sun, bareheaded, alone among strangers. We brought silvery roses from Derrynavglaun and anguish and remorse. Charles died on the Fourth of July. It was perfect, if brutal, timing for this quintessential American who so often quoted the dying John Adams, 'Thomas Jefferson lives … ', Mr. Adams not knowing Mr. Jefferson, too, would die before that July 4, 1826 was out. Charles' death in the impersonal surroundings of New York City–Cornell University Hospital attended by doctors, who, after months of tests, were unable to provide a correct diagnosis of his illness, is a testament to the capricious virtues of modern medicine. We do not know why, for the two years following his open heart surgery, despite sophisticated tests and a covey of medical experts, doctors could chart Charles' decline but could do nothing to halt it.

June 18, 1997

Dear Pat—

Something is terribly wrong with me and they can't figure out what. After cat-scans and a variety of cardio-grams, they agree it's not lung cancer or heart trouble or blood clot. So they're putting me in the hospital today to concentrate on infectious diseases. I am getting worse, barely able to get out of bed, but still have high hopes for recovery … if only I can get a diagnosis! Curiouser and curiouser! I'll keep you informed.

I'll have the lawyer visit the hospital to be sure you inherit the rest of the place in MT. if it comes to that.

I send love to you & Shannon. Hope things are better there!

Love,
C.

Charles was buried in the old cemetery on the University of North Carolina campus at Chapel Hill. The day before he died he dictated a letter from his hospital bed for his old friend, Bill Friday, President Emeritus of the university, asking for help in locating a burial plot. He wrote that he was groggy and out of it, but didn't think he was dying, adding a handwritten postscript: 'I am only now beginning to appreciate the love I have for Chapel Hill. It is a moving place the more I think about it. And you have made it so. C.' The measured pace and thoughtful reflection at Chapel Hill, the civilized discourse, was balm for Charles' splintered spirit. But Andy Rooney doubts Charles will hang around Chapel Hill long: 'I know Charles … And I know he won't be content there either.'

The day of the funeral, a somber, black-clad throng gathered under a dark canvas awning. Petie Baird was there, not pausing in her distress, as she rushed past us. Charles' older daughter Lisa, who while still in college so delighted him one evening by arriving for dinner in a chic Diane Von

Furstenberg print, sat with her sister, Susan. At the start of her career, Susan had driven Charles crazy with worry when she insisted on living in a walk-up flat on one of New York's meaner streets. Charles' beautiful sister, Catherine, was there, of course, as was his younger brother, Wallace.

Izzy Bleckman, whose unhappy divorce diverted Charles and me from our own reality, sat close by. Charles' collaborator on *North Carolina Is My Home,* Loonis McClohan, accepted his place under the awning. Bill Friday, a member of the Democratic cabal which urged Charles to run for the North Carolina Senate seat against the mean-spirited Jesse Helms, paid homage. Ironically, it was Dan Rather who endured the southern heat standing, shaken but uncomplaining, at our side.

A cortege of limousines carried the mourners to a memorial service celebrating Charles' life. I paced the grass surround in which the coffin lay under a mantle of red roses, weeping, as J.R. reached out and took one hand of each of his sisters, escorting them up the aisle to the front of the auditorium, where he seated them in the row marked 'FAMILY.'

For Charles, I have two regrets.

Time stopped before he wrote what he longed to write, an epic poem for Lewis and Clark, ' ... and they heard the meadowlark sing.' Charles spoke often in those last years of wanting to write something that would live. It was to be the tale of those men who paused for a moment not far from the Montana cabin and then 'proceeded on.' We built the schoolhouse for the poem's manger, but the old building stands, weather-beaten, devoid of life.

When months went by and our overtures to friends, family and colleagues alike were rebuffed, and we heard not a single word from anyone on the East Coast, Shannon turned to me with a lament, 'What kind of people did he run around with back there?' I have had cause to ask that question myself since Charles died. Which is my second regret. No one stepped forward to defend this man, when, after death, he was attacked by those who had not the courage to attack while he was alive. Tabloids, talk shows, comedians found plenty to say about Charles and me. Best friends, admiring peers, family members, said nothing at all. What fragment of Charles, I wonder, did they hold so lightly that it could be so cavalierly tossed aside. Passionate about life, trapped in a cross-current of conflicting obligations, Charles, as he said so often and so wearily, had done the best he could. We all have our own demons. Charles Kuralt, inclusive, tolerant, amused, without malice or pettiness, slow to anger, quick to absolve, lived with his demons better than most.

For myself, I'll not add up the regrets, but content myself with Charles' coda. Life is not simple. We never completed our goodbyes. We rushed to meet, refused to meet, argued, parted, came back together. I didn't see him before he died. I was in Ireland when, on the day he entered the hospital, he wrote to me that last letter, its sad, shaky handwriting punishment enough for all our wrongs, real or imagined.

Charles called the cabin on the Valentine's Day before his death, reminding me of a radio piece to be aired on NPR, Loonis McGlohon playing the piano, Charles rolling out the lyrics of Cole Porter, George Gershwin, Rogers and Hart. He paused for a moment; then, for one last time, music filled the cabin on the Big Hole:

I opened the blind
and looked through the crack
at the track leading back to you,
and what did I do?
I thought about you.

They want my place, I said, flushing with anger. The young woman from the Bureau of Land Management looked at me in astonishment. Of course, they want your place. I want your place. Everyone wants your place.

There was no arguing with that.

After Charles' funeral, Kathleen returned to Reno to guide her clients through the perils of our legal system. Shannon flew off to assume the considerably less vexing task of tending the Derrynavglaun animals. The girls left J.R. to deal with me. We drove the Blue Ridge as Charles and I used to do, stopping where we stopped. J.R. stalled for time until, worn down, I agreed to the children's cacophonous demands that I not go to the cabin but wait in Ireland until we were able to meet with— who?—someone, we didn't know who.

We were lurching along that dull, doubtful path grief opens after a sudden death, trying for a family reconciliation with the clan, some of whom we had met briefly, some not at all. We were stopped in our tracks when Charles' estate, unexpectedly and inexplicably, fired his legal firm, hiring lawyers who appeared to believe their duty compelled them to lay bare our personal lives. In a few short weeks, those boys succeeded in making a public mockery of Petie Baird's marriage, sullying Charles' reputation and destroying any chance of rapprochement among those whom he loved. The estate's lawyers wanted, said they were going to get, everything Charles and I shared. It was a dreadful thing to do, a mistake I thought then and still think now. The reaction of our Montana neighbors to all of this was as heartwarming as one of Charles' On The Road stories.

Our town's late high school basketball coach was once asked where the hell Twin Bridges was. He replied it was between the Dairy Queen and the Exxon station. His siting is no longer technically accurate since the Dairy Queen closed, but the image his playful answer suggests holds true. Twin is the hub of a small, blue-jeaned, ranching community, enlivened during the summer months by schools of fishermen splashing slivers of silver. This quiet and conservative community, equally unexpectedly and inexplicably, circled the wagons when the estate lawyers struck.

It happened one hot August day as I was languishing in Conamara waiting for someone from the estate to return our calls. A neighbor upstream of the cabin, one of the summer people in town to collect his mail, mentioned in casual conversation with the postmaster that someone was at the schoolhouse. Everyone in Twin Bridges knew I was in Ireland. Eyebrows raised. Questions asked. Kathleen called. J.R. notified. The sheriff alerted. Pick-ups and dogs and people nosed around the schoolhouse bluff. There were 'aw shuckses' and booted toes kicking aimlessly in the dirt. The pony-tailed stranger leaning coolly against the schoolhouse door ignored proffered introductions. The outcome was an estate lock on the schoolhouse door and a new padlock on the gate. The vigilance of my neighbors secured the cabin.

Thanks to them, when I arrived in the early hours of the morning after a disheveled flight from Derrynavglaun, I was able to lie, albeit sleepless, in my own bed.

I didn't fare so well a few mornings after my arrival. I glanced up at the schoolhouse, while putting out grain for the whitetails, to see furniture being loaded into a gaudy-colored rental truck. An estate lawyer returned with a couple who once kept an eye on the place. The three methodically stripped the schoolhouse of the antique partners' desk, the Chinese rug, the river painting and everything else worth more than a quarter. J.R., at the cabin for the day to see how I was doing, did his best to restrain me. His best was not good enough. A ridiculous scene ensued. It was the sort of confrontation that used to make Charles' stomach roil and his jaw clinch before he waded into the fray with that tightly controlled air of reasonable compromise. Reasonable compromise always hits me on the second day. I am coiled ready to strike on the first.

With the Jeep blocking the rental truck, we prowled and growled around each other like coyotes over a dead carcass. The lawyer shouted at J.R. J.R. shouted at me. I shouted at the local couple. A sheriff's deputy sat in his pick-up watching with unconcealed ennui. Every few minutes someone leaped into a vehicle, speeding to the nearest available telephone, returning with new orders or insults or simply because there was no place else to go. My brilliant Bozeman attorney, Jim Goetz, advised me in a series of agitated, inchoate telephone calls to forego this unseemly behavior. I stood aside, watching the truck labor down the rutted, dirt road, not it or its contents to be seen again.

After I filed papers with the court contesting the estate's claim to the Montana property, I retreated to Derrynavglaun. By ducking out, I missed the comical response to a rush of reporters darting in and out of Twin Bridges' main street shops eager for scandalous tidbits. Freshly minted T-shirts began appearing with the question PAT WHO? in bold shamrock green across the front. Folks who knew me said they didn't, and folks who didn't said they did. I am sorry I missed it.

Conamara, it turned out, was not, as I always believed, the perfect place to hide out. A free lancer, a shiny sophisticate, flitted over from London and settled down before the roaring fire at Ballynahinch Castle prepared to flush me out. She and a photographer ventured down our bog road two or three times a day, put their cell phone on automatic and waited for me to come shrieking out of the house. The furthest I ventured was a nose through the drapes. The experience of helplessness was enough to make me sympathetic to the Waco casualties who suffered far worse at the hands of the FBI. The obliging Ballynahinch staff presented her with a copy of *The Man Who Stayed Home*. With that she was off to more fertile ground. She drove out to Carna, finding a village delighted I had been caught out but with little to offer her in the way of gossip. Pauraic O'Cualain, the foil of my Conamara memoir, was gleeful, repeating each time he saw me, 'You write about me. They write about you.'

Springtime brought me back to Montana, to hear after a wrenching two days of testimony, the Madison County district judge deny us a full hearing. He issued a summary judgment in favor of the estate. The judgment included my Jeep. Twin took it in stride. We could get you a canoe, someone suggested. You can float down the Big Hole and hitch back. A bicycle was offered. Good exercise. Maybe, you could hoist a flag when you need supplies. Cars passing down Burma Road could drop 'em off en route. When the estate picked up the Jeep, Twin Bridges had a surprise for me. As I watched my transport disappear over the hill past the schoolhouse, a dusty white Bronco came in sight. Its driver executed a sharp left at my gate. He pulled up smartly in the middle of the cabin clearing and jumped out. My neighbors had brought me a car. By way of explanation, one of them pointed out I would be more trouble than I was worth if they were forced to worry about whether or not I was out of milk. Waiting for the Montana courts to straighten things out, friends brought fresh lettuces and tomatoes in the summer. Eggs in the fall. Cooked me dinner at my house and at theirs. Offered me a Scotch before dinner and a kiss on the cheek after. Their kindnesses kept me out of the river.

All that is yesterday. I squint at tomorrow.

Dividing my time these past fifteen years between the cabin and Derrynavglaun, I have long since left the city behind me. I say to any who ask, I am a country woman myself. Charles and I became aware of the transformation some years ago when the shadow of a bald eagle, dark against the snow, no longer distracted me, but the drone of a twin-engine plane made me stop and scan the sky. In a quiet Montana January, it is sound that attracts. When I heard a raucous goose's call early one morning, I followed it as if it were the Pied Piper's strain.

There she sat below our bridge, her long neck stretched like a slide trombone, her despair vibrating in the still air. The creek was freezing over, snow trembled on every blade of grass, she was starving, and, no, she would not go gentle into that good night. At first, I took her to be a wild thing. I timidly threw handfuls of grain down onto the ice. 'Ah, Bon Amie, don't be afraid.' She wasn't afraid. Flapping her wings feebly, she slid, waddled, crawled over to me, complaining the whole way. As the grain rained down on her, she sat, splat, in the middle of it, gobbling it up.

By the next afternoon, she was reconnoitering, climbing slantwise up the creek bank. She perused the yard, ate copious amounts of grain, gulped water from a red bucket, preened. She followed me around, chattering constantly about her adventures. If I went inside, she walked the perimeter of the cabin, arching her neck, peering in the low windows. Spying me, she would arrange herself on the ground, tuck her head into her feathers, coyly watch me out of one eye. Each evening at sunset disdaining the bed of hay under the front porch, she waddled, clucking, back to the tatter of open water. Anxiously, I would call after her, 'Goodnight, Bon Amie. Wake me if the coyote comes.'

'Mom,' the kids moaned when I told them about her, 'you are going crazy.' Well, perhaps, but that big, brown goose standing on one leg, her head turning inquisitively at the sound of my voice, made me inordinately happy. Reluctantly, I began asking neighbors about Bon Amie. I called the game warden, the bird rescue lady, the local naturalist. I drove the dirt road up and down the river. 'Did anyone loose a big brown, goose, the sweetest goose? No, really.' And, darned if I didn't find Bon Amie's owner. The previous June when the river flooded its banks, Bon Amie, paddling in the slough that ran through her ranch, had floated out on the tide. A neighbor boy reported seeing her mostly dead, from a coyote attack, he thought. A rancher up river watched her swimming at the edge of his pasture till the cold came. It took six months, thirty miles and untold dangers for fate to drop Bon Amie onto my doorstep.

She's back home now with her mate. Still, love lingers and with it an amorphous longing, an embryonic discontent with my life on the Big Hole. It is a haven but not quite. The river has changed, busy now in the fine months, thick with guides and fishermen casting Blue Winged Olives and Lee Wulff Grays toward the front porch steps. Piercing lights rip the velvet fabric of the night. The road churns up low sworls of dust as trucks towing boat trailers speed by leaving dead animals in their wake, a rabbit here, a deer there. Gunshot disturbs the crisp fall air as the wild things and I tense in quiet dread.

In a time when it is impossible to protect the things one loves, I muse whether it is possible to offer a moment of grace. I remember an old couple I met on an early trip to Ireland. She was the widow of the captain of the *Asgard*, a ship that smuggled guns into Howth for the 1916 Easter Uprising. He was an Austrian émigré. They were devout Christians, Protestants, who chided me for declaring a bent toward religious skepticism as unbecoming arrogance. Their backgrounds, hers an old-line Republican ethos, his grounded in battle with the Nazis, steeped them in the sanctity of the safe house. They vowed no one seeking asylum would ever be turned away.

I thought of Bon Amie, of Charles' pheasant and my spotted fawn. A plan began to take shape. Man needs little protecting here in Montana. It is the animal kingdom that is under siege. I will try to make good on our promise, Charles' and mine. For as long as I can, I'll keep this one hundred and ten acres as a a place where the wild things can sit a spell and enjoy life. We—the White-tailed Deer (*Odocoileus virginianus*) and the Sandhill Crane (*Crus canadensis*) and the Mountain Pack Rat (*Neotoma cinera*) and Bon Amie (genus unknown) if she should ever take it into her head to again go rambling—will take our ease here at the newly christened Bluebird Wildlife Sanctuary.

Not long ago I invited a few old friends to a dedication ceremony up at the schoolhouse. We munched Grannysmith apples smeared with Roquefort cheese and nibbled slices of *Quiche à la Tomate, Nicoise.* We toasted the wild creatures with glasses of Trefethen Cabernet. We finished off with a platter of Viennese Crescents. The menu was one of Charles' from the halcyon days.

I hope for a more formal dedication in a year or two with a chamber music concert at the schoolhouse in honor of those men Charles admired, Meriwether Lewis and William Clark who 'heard the meadowlark sing'. Maybe, I'll see you there.

DATELINE AMERICA

APACHE, OKLAHOMA. This country has too many chiefs and not enough Indians. I speak as a Kiowa myself. I was standing in a corner at a Kiowa war dance, reporting the homecoming of a couple of U.S. army warriors, when suddenly the dance ended and I heard my name mentioned, followed by war whoops. Somebody put a blanket over my shoulders. A lean and angry-looking man said, 'Dance.'

'I can't dance,' I said. Somebody thrust a fan into one of my hands and a rattle into the other.

'We are turning you into a Kiowa,' the angry-looking man said.

'Dance.'

'I don't even do the foxtrot well,' I said.

'Dance,' he said.

I danced. At either side of me were other large and muscular Kiowas in warpaint, dancing like mad. I felt compelled to smile, but nobody else was smiling. The compulsion to smile left me.

At length, at great length, the drums stopped. An old man named Cecil Horse, son of Hunting Horse, a Custer scout, made a speech in English and pronounced my Indian name: Blue Eagle. More banging of drums and whooping. I stood as erect and eaglelike as I could and tried to get used to the idea of being Blue Eagle while old man Horse made the same speech in Kiowa. When he got to the name part, there was a murmur in the room. He called me over. 'I said it wrong in English,' he said, embarrassed. 'You are Bluebird, not Blue Eagle.' As he tried to tell me this, his elderly wife kept shouting into his bad ear, 'It's too late! You've already pronounced it! It's too late!' 'It's too late,' old man Horse said to me, 'but you are Bluebird, not Blue Eagle.' I told him that suited me better anyway.

Then the drums started again, and the chanting, and I felt proud, like Crazy Horse after the Little Big Horn. I turned to Izzy Bleckman, the cameraman with whom I work, and said, 'Gee, last week they made me a Kentucky Colonel, and this week they've made me a Kiowa Indian.'

Izzy said, 'You are working your way up to Jew.'